Book Marketing Fundamentals

Hank Quense

No one buys a book they never heard of. You have to tell people about your book before they can buy it.

Book Marketing Fundamentals contains a comprehensive inventory of essential marketing tasks and explanations on why you should use them and how to use them. The book is written specifically for first-time authors searching for a way to market their book.

Reviews for Creating Stories:

Joylene Butler: Author of Matowak Women Who Cries: This book is a true treasure and needs to be in the library of every writer worldwide.
Indie Reader: CREATING STORIES is a useful resource for new writers who have a terrific story idea but aren't sure how to go about turning that into a functional, readable, enjoyable novel
Mark Henderson: British author of Cruel and Unusual Punnishment. I recommend Creating Stories unreservedly to fiction writers everywhere.

Reviews for How to Self-publish and Market a Book

Dani C.: This guide is amazing. As a brand new author diving into self-publishing I found this book to be thorough and well laid out.
Joseph Wyrick: . . is a "how-to" manual for authors who want to sell their work. Quense, who has written a number of books himself, has taken what he has learned from his own publishing experiences and put that information into this guide.© 2020 Hank Quense

ISBN: 978-1733342445
Published in the United States of America.
Published by Strange Worlds Publishing

Table of Contents

Foreword

For a new author, marketing is a vague, bewildering concept. The process of writing a book does nothing to prepare an author for the necessary chores of marketing that book. Marketing is a daunting project that all authors must face. The scariest part about marketing is the plethora of choices and tactics that are possible to include in a marketing campaign. It's like the author must cross a vast swampland without a map. And the swamp is filled with alligators otherwise known as scam artists. And then there are all the false paths and dead ends.

What's an author to do? How does she navigate the swamp and retain her sanity? *The answer is to find a mentor, a guide.* That's my job. I've crossed the swampland a number of times. I've lost a few toes to the alligators and I know where the dead ends are.

So get in the boat with me and let's start rowing.

The marketing tactics described in this book will change depending upon which of three scenarios your book falls into:

- ☐ Your book was put out by a publishing company
- ☐ You self-published your book and it is currently available
- ☐ You plan to self-publish your book but it isn't yet available.

Chapter 1: Getting Started

The ideal time to begin your marketing efforts is several months before your book becomes available. However, if your book is already out, don't worry. You can still market the book. Actually, it is never too early or too late to start your marketing campaign.

Most chapters in the book will have a number of activities to work on. In total, there are more than sixty marketing activities or informational sections. You don't need to work on them all. You, in your role as the book's marketing director, will have to decide which ones to implement and which ones to ignore. Since some of the activities will require funding, part of your decision making will have a financial element to it. Another factor is whether the book has a print or an ebook edition. A few of the activities will not be suitable for a print book and others won't apply to an ebook. If you have both print and ebook editions, then all of the marketing tasks will apply to your book.

A word of caution: don't look at the sheer number of activities and panic. They all don't have to be worked on immediately. There is nothing wrong with spacing out your marketing over a long period. It would be a mistake to go into overload trying to complete all the activities in as short a time as possible. You can and should go through the lists and choose the ones that look easy. Start with those. Other activities may require the investment of a chunk of time because you'll have investigate how to do it and it may also involve a bit of learning before you can start it.

My assigning a task or activity to a specific area such as Platform or Marketing Content is more than a bit arbitrary. Where a task is slotted isn't all that important. The grouping simply makes it easier for me to deal with the large number of activities.

If you have, or will have, a publisher, it will (or should) perform some of the pre-launch activities. The publisher may (or may not) choose to work on the post-launch marketing activities. How do you know which activities are pre-launch and which ones are not? You can use the extensive spreadsheet I developed. Besides indicating the ideal time frame, the spreadsheet can be used to control your marketing campaign. It shows every marketing task listed in this book and is available in .numbers (for Mac) and .xls (for PCs) formats. To get a copy send me an email at hanque99 (at) gmail (dot) com. Specify which format you want. A screen shot of the spreadsheet is pasted below.

Book Marketing Plan © 2020 Hank Quense						
Task	Mandatory/ Optional	Part of marketing plan?	Ideal time frame	Budget Item?	Estimated costs	Percent complete
Platform						
Website	Mandatory	Yes	Pre-launch	yes		0
Amazon Central Page	Mandatory	Yes	Pre-launch	no	na	0
Social media accounts						
Goodreads	Mandatory	Yes	Pre-launch	no	na	0
Twitter	Optional	Yes	Pre-launch	no	na	0
Facebook	Optional	Yes	Pre-launch	no	na	0
LinkedIn	Optional	Yes	Pre-launch	no	na	0
Strategic Marketing Plan	Mandatory	Yes	Pre-launch	no	na	0
Media kit	Mandatory	Yes	Pre-launch	no	na	0
Marketing Content						
Book Blurb	Mandatory	Yes	Pre-launch	no	na	0

If you have a publisher, it will be in your best interest to determine exactly which marketing activities it will be responsible for.

Although the publisher will take care of the pre-launch stuff, it is important for you to understand what those tasks are so you can better discuss them with the publisher.

So let's get to the crux of the matter. You probably have questions that need to be answered. Does book marketing work? Is it worth the time and money?

The answer to both questions is a definitive yes and/or maybe.

To explain the last statement, book marketing is similar to playing the lottery. If you buy a lottery ticket, you have a small, very small, chance to win a lot of money. If you don't buy a ticket, you have no chance of winning the money. With book marketing, if you do the marketing stuff, you have a small, very small, chance of making a lot of money through your royalties. If you don't do the marketing, you have zero chance of making money on the book.

With the lottery, you can also win smaller amounts of cash. So too with book marketing. If you market the book, you may earn back your marketing investment through your royalties and perhaps a bit more.

So the real question is this: Will you market your book? If the answer is 'Yes', read on.

There are seven areas to be worked on. Here are brief descriptions of each.

- Platform: Refers to you and your book. It's your author brand.
- Marketing Content: Is material you write up about the book. Most of it will be used in other activities.
- Marketing Activities: Is work you will do to tell others about your book
- Book Reviews: Is activity to increase the number of book reviews your book gets.
- Events: Are activities in which you participate, either physically or virtually.
- Publicity: Is telling the world about your book.
- Advertising: Is just what you think it is.

So let's get started! You can do this!

Chapter 2: Platform

Introduction

To start your marketing project, let's establish a platform for your book and your author persona. If this is your first foray into book marketing, these activities will take some time, but they are worth the time and effort.

The contents of this chapter are listed below.

- ☐ Strategic Marketing Plan
- ☐ Website page
- ☐ Amazon Central
- ☐ Social media accounts
- ☐ Media kit

Most of these activities can't be completed until your book is either published or is in pre-order. In other words, after it has a presence on the internet. You'll need the cover image and other information about the book before you can complete these activities. If you have a publisher, a few activities may already be done, but you should review them with an eye to improve and strengthen them.

Strategic Marketing Plan

The Strategic Marketing Plan is the genesis of all your marketing activities. It is the master plan that directs all the tactical tasks that you decide to use. If this sounds nebulous, let me rephrase it. All the marketing tasks except the strategic plan are tactical ones. All these tactical tasks add up to build your tactical plan. Your tactical plan must be agreement with the objectives in your strategic plan. If the tactical plans and the strategic plan don't agree, some of your marketing activities will be a waste of time. And possibly money. A marketing task shouldn't be used just because it's doable; it should be used because it agrees with the strategic plan.

Your strategic marketing plan will require a bit of thinking and decision making on your part. Save the answers to your plan; it's reusable for your next book.

Your responses to the strategic plan will vary depending upon the status of your book. More about that later.

I developed a spreadsheet to record your answers. It even has sample answers to make your life a bit simpler. To get a copy, send me an email hanque99 (at) gmail (dot) com. It's available in .xls or .numbers formats.

Some of the answers to the questions require information developed later on. As a consequence, you may not be able to immediately complete the strategic plan That's okay as long as the plan is fully developed before you start spending money on the marketing efforts. This is because the strategic plan is your marketing roadmap and it will define which marketing tactics you deploy.

Here is an outline of your plan. I'll explain much more after the outline.

Marketing Plan: Product, Customers and Competitors:

- Describe the book.
- What's different about the book?
- What benefit does the customer get from buying your book?
- Why would a customer buy your book instead of a competitor's book?
- Who are your competitors?
- What benefits does their books offer?

- How is your book better than the competitors' book?
- Who are your target customers?
- What sales channels will you use to sell your book?
- What marketing channels will you use to reach your targeted customers?
- What will you price your book at?
- How does your price compare to the competitors' price?

Marketing Plan: Objectives and Budgets:
- What are the financial objectives for this plan?
- How will you measure these financial results?
- What are the secondary objectives for this plan?
- How will you measure the results?
- What is your marketing budget for year 1?
- What is your marketing budget for year 2?

Explanations for the terms follow.

Describe the book

This isn't as easy as you may first think. Don't write down a superficial answer. Get into what the book is *really* about. However, keep it short. This doesn't call for a synopsis and it may require a number of rewrites before it's done.

What's different about the book?

This question is critically important. Later on, you'll use the answers to develop an important marketing message called the book blurb.

Who are your competitors?

The competitor questions will require research. This is easiest done on Amazon or another web-based book seller. It can also be done in a book store. (But you'll have to be sneaky as you jot down notes.)

Who are your target customers?

Let's talk in more detail about the identification of customers. The first step in the development of a marketing plan is to identify who the customers are and what problem your book will solve for those customers.

Once you stop groaning, I will proceed.

If you have written a non-fiction book, you must have had a set of potential readers in mind. For instance, if you have written a book about fixing household plumbing, your potential readers are people who live in homes with leaky faucets or pipes. Or people who suspect they will have leak problems someday. Your customers are the plumbing-needy and your book will solve the customers 'needs for plumbing advice.

If you wrote a book about how to do surgery at home on the kitchen table, your target readership is a bit more limited. Possibly it'll be folks who don't have health insurance although I'm not sure this book will solve the customers' problem. It may actually worsen their problem.

If you wrote a children's picture book, you may think the kids are the customers: they aren't. Kids don't have money or credit cards. Kids don't browse bookstores or websites. Your customers are the parents and grandparents. Other family members and close friends are also customers.

If your book is a fictional tale, you have to position it depending upon the potential audience. Romance readers are quite different from mystery fans and so are sci-fi aficionados. In either case, your book will entertain the reader which is a way of solving a problem for the customer. It gives them a break from reality.

Once you identify your readership, the rest of the marketing plan will be aimed at that group of people, not the general population.

What sales channels will you use to sell your book?

Typical sales channels are Amazon, Barnes & Noble, book stores, etc. Your publisher will have a lot to do with this and the actually selection may be out of your hands. Nevertheless, you have to know the sales channels that will be used.

What marketing channels will you use to reach your targeted customers?

Marketing channels refer primarily the social media sites you will use to reach the customers.

What will you price your book at?

How you price the book will have a large impact on book sales and your royalties. A publisher will take care of this item.

How does your price compare to the competitors price?

I'll discuss these last 2 question together. First, a few words of advice. Don't let your ego get in the way of making a rational decision on this subject. It's true you may have spent years producing this masterpiece and you think the book's value is enormous and that thousands of readers will be happy to pay a premium price to get a chance to own their very own copy. Well, you're wrong. You are an unknown author and unknown authors can't command premium prices. It'll be hard enough selling your book without the added burden of an unrealistically high price.

Back to the question on how to come up with the price. The answer is research. Let's consider print books first. The best place to do this research is on Amazon or some other major book site, although you can do this in a book store or even a library. Once on the site, search for books that are similar to yours. If your book is non-fiction and covers plumbing repairs, search for other plumbing repair books. Note the price for the ones that have similar subject matter and a similar number of pages. That is the target price of your book. If your research reveals four similar print books and their prices range from $15.99 to $24.99, your book should be priced somewhere within that range. You can also make a pricing decision to make your book available at a lower price if you wish.

If your book is fiction, search for other books within your genre. This may be a tougher job than with the non-fiction books. Genre books have superstar authors who command premium prices. Ignore them. You don't have the clout to demand a premium price — yet.

Your search should be for lesser known authors in your genre. If your print book has three-hundred pages, you should search for other similar genre books with three-hundred pages, approximately. Comparing your three-hundred page book to a six-hundred page one isn't very productive. The six-hundred page print book will cost more to produce because of the larger number of pages and subsequent production costs, so that book will require a higher price than a three-hundred page print book. Set your price to get the best possible sales at your current status as a new author.

For an ebook, the search process is similar but you'll probably come up with a confusing array of data. A bit of explanation is in order. There is a debate going on about ebook pricing. Many voices claim that ebooks sell best if they're priced at $0.99. Others contend that a higher price yields more profits but fewer sales. There are studies that conclude the sweet spot for an ebook is $2.99 to $5.99. Obviously, an ebook selling for $2.99 will bring in more revenue for an author that an ebook selling at $0.99. On the other hand, an ebook selling for $.99 could sell more books than a higher priced ebook. You can ask for advice on web sites like LinkedIn and you'll get replies, many of them contradictory. After reading the replies, it still comes down to you making a decision. Make sure this is a business decision.

Another complicating factor is the presence of best-selling authors. Their ebooks come from the major publishing houses. Their price will be closer to $10.00 or even higher. It will not even be close to $.99. Here again, the premium price is due to name recognition and clout. If you price your ebook close to $10.00 you won't have to worry about tracking sales; you won't get any. A first-time self-published author simply can't expect to use premium pricing and sell any books, no matter how great the content is.

Here is my pricing strategy. For my novels, I start out at $3.99 for ebook and $19.99 for print. As the book ages, I'll drop the ebook price lower.

For non-fiction, I initially price a multi-topic ebook at $5.99. Some of my non-fiction books are dedicated to a smaller topic and I price them at $2.99.

Marketing Plan Objectives

I'll address all of these questions together. Another early step in market plan development is to establish a set of financial objectives. A business needs to set goals for itself and if you haven't realized it yet, let me point out that once you publish a book, you own a business and the purpose of this business is to market and sell your book.

The reality facing a first-time self-published author is that you won't sell many books in the near term even though, over time, you may indeed sell truckloads of books. For this reason, you should establish goals that recognize this reality and keep your initial goals modest.

While a business may have non-financial goals, they are secondary to the financial goals. Such goals can be: get interviewed on a local radio or TV show; have a book signing in a book store.

An important consideration is that the objectives must be measurable. Another consideration is that they must be reasonable and achievable. Setting goals that can't be reached is simply an exercise in futility. However, the goals must be hard enough to reach that they will force you to turn off the TV and work on meeting the goals.

Next, let's discuss how the strategic marketing plan changes depending upon the book's situation.

Scenario 1: Your book was put out by a publishing company.

In this case, much of the work was (or should have been) done by the publisher. The publisher will establish the price and the sales channels. It will target the book to an appropriate set of customers. It may start an Amazon Central page in your name. It also probably started an author page for you on its website.

While this relieves you some responsibilities, you should check the Amazon page to strengthen the publisher's material and add more content to it. You also want your own web site in addition to the publisher's web page.

Scenario 2: You self-published your book and it is currently available.

As part of the self-publishing process, you have already established the sales channels such as Kindle or Smashwords. You also uploaded descriptive material about the book and established a price. After you finish working on the strategic marketing plan, you should review what you did when you published the book. Possibly that content can be strengthened. You should also reconsider your pricing strategy.

Scenario 3: You plan to self-publish your book but it isn't yet available.

All of the strategic marketing plan applies to this scenario.

Website Page

As a new author, you have to face the fact your book is published in the 21st century. Readers search for and find books by using the internet. The implication of the last statement is that you and your book need a website. The simplest way to establish a web presence is to use a program like Wordpress or Blogger or Weebly.

Blogger can be found at https://www.blogger.com/about/?r=2. It is an app from Google and is fairly simple to use. You can find Weebly at https://www.weebly.com

Wordpress comes in two versions. One, Wordpress.com, uses a Wordpress server that is common to many, many bloggers and the second, Wordpress.org, uses a server that you rent from a service provider. In this latter case, you have to decide on a host server and obtain a domain name.

The shared version of Wordpress uses a combined URL like http://wordpress/your name. The other version of Wordpress requires you to buy a domain name to establish your own website. Whichever Wordpress version you use, you can build a complete website with it including a blog. My website hankquense.org/wp uses Wordpress. I use the second type of Wordpress, the one that isn't shared with others.

Websites such as Wordpress, Blogger and Weebly have two essential types of content: pages and posts. Pages are static in that they don't change unless you deliberately set out to change them. Once you establish a page on the website, it stays there, doesn't move and doesn't change.

Posts are for blogging and these aren't static like pages. A new blog post will appear at the top of the website once you publish it. When you write a second post, the initial one will move down to make room for the new post.

So what do you do with a website once you have it up and running? You use it to pimp your book. There should be a dedicated page for the book and it should be easy to find. Don't make a visitor search for the book page.

Initially that page should have a picture of the cover, your book blurb and buy links. You can also put your short synopsis on it.

Use your blog to write blog posts. The blog posts can be about anything: your grandkids, writing anecdotes, vacation plans and pictures. The important thing is to issue blog posts periodically so that people will build up an interest in the blog and revisit it. It will be important to write blog posts about the book also. Tell the readers why you wrote the book, what problems you had to overcome, what you liked about the process. You can also interview your characters.

If this section on blogging doesn't make sense to you, I'd advise you to invest in a book on blogging. Or you can watch training videos. Wordpress has a library of these videos. So do the other website options. Or, you can search YouTube to find more instructional videos.

No matter how you come about getting your website, once it's up and running, ***use it!*** Start writing blogs and post material about your book.

Amazon Central

Once your book is available for sale or pre-order on Amazon, you can start an Author Page. If you have a publisher, it may have started this page for you. In this case, you should look at it to see if you can add content to it.

You'll find Author Central at:

https://authorcentral.amazon.com/gp/home

After you start your author page, you can add your bio and other information to the page. One of the great features of the Author Page is you can add a wealth of information about the book that you couldn't do when you uploaded it to Kindle.

The book topics include *Editorial Reviews*. These are reviews that Amazon won't allow to be posted on the book site because Amazon won't allow paid reviews. If you receive a review from a prestigious site like *Publishers Weekly,* this is the place to post it.

Another topic is *From the Author*. Here you tell readers why you wrote the book. Or the problems you encountered in writing it. Or anecdotes from the writing process.

You can also upload videos to the page (i.e. a trailer) and you can set up an RSS feed so your blog posts show up on the Author Page.

Taken together, the Author Page is a great marketing tool.

A FAQs page about Author Central can be found at: https://authorcentral.amazon.com/gp/help?ie=UTF8&topicID=200799 660#emailsig

I suggest you make the Author Page link part of your email signature.   Email signatures will be discussed under Marketing Content.

For what an author's page looks like, go to mine:

https://www.amazon.com/-/e/B002BM76IE

Media Kit

The purpose of a media kit is to let folks in the media and other interested parties know about your writing credentials. If the book is your only writing project so far, there won't be a lot of material, but start it anyway. If you published short stories, articles or other content, add it to plump up your resumé. The media kit lives on your website or blog and must be available to anyone who wants to download it. For that reason, you may want to consider not putting personal information in it like your home address, or your phone number.

So, what goes into a media kit? Here is a list of items that make up your kit:

- ☐ Bio.
- ☐ Press releases.
- ☐ Website links.
- ☐ Body of work.
- ☐ Book descriptions.
- ☐ Book reviews.

Make sure the media kit is a doc or pdf file so it can be downloaded and opened by everyone.

As long as we're discussing the media kit contents, it's a good time to write your bio. Write two bios, a long one of a page or two and a short one, a single paragraph or two. The long one goes in the media kit and the short one can be used in guest posts on blogs and in other places.

Bios are written in third person, not first person. Include your photo in the bio and make sure it's a good picture. Preferably, you should be smiling. Don't use a picture in which you are frowning, glaring, snarling or otherwise looking unfriendly or hostile. You don't want to scare away potential customers.

Social Media Accounts

Social media is an essential part of your marketing plan and your branding. However, be warned. Social media is a major time suck and many sites are next to worthless when it comes to marketing and selling your book. Nevertheless, you must persist.

I'll assume you don't have these accounts and that you are not familiar with social media generally.

Create a Goodreads Account

Goodreads is a place for readers and authors to interact. You can find it by using this link: https://www.goodreads.com.

The great thing about the readers on this site is that many of them write book reviews. Once you have your account set up, start using it by joining the author program. This will enable you to establish an author page with a bio, book listings and other information. You'll find the author program here:
https://www.goodreads.com/author/program

After you get the book cover and develop the blurb and short synopsis for your soon-to-be released book, add them to Goodreads and list the expected publication date. If your book sounds interesting (i.e. you have added compelling material), other members will start to list the book as 'want to read.' Send a 'friend request 'to those members because your Goodreads friends will get a message when you post a review, run a book sale or schedule an event.

Goodreads has numerous groups covering just about every conceivable aspect of reading and publishing books. Join a few of these groups and participate in the threads. You can schedule events such as a book launch and send a message to your friends about the event.

Goodreads is one of the better social media sites.

Another site for readers and authors is Librarything, but it isn't as robust as Goodreads. You can find it here: https://www.librarything.com

Create a FaceBook Account

You may already have a Facebook account; it seems most people do. If so, what you have is called a personal account. If you don't have one, go to https://www.facebook.com and start a personal account.

Facebook also has an option called 'Pages 'and you want one, but you can't start it until after you have a personal account. Pages can be started for businesses, music groups, community groups and even authors. You can start one for your book or, better yet, start it for yourself as an author. That way you can add information about your second book without starting another page.

Once you start the page, add your book cover, your book blurb and new reviews as you get them. On your page you'll have the ability to post content similar to the way a blog operates. Use this feature to post new reviews and other content.

On your personal account, ask friends to like the page. This will increase the number of potential buyers who see the page.

Establish a Twitter Account

Twitter is quite different from the previous social media sites discussed. You can find Twitter here: https://twitter.com

On Twitter, you post short messages that are 280 characters or less. There are a lot of authors and writers on Twitter, and you should spend time finding ones that write in your genre and connect with them.

You can post tweets (as they're called) on just about any possible topic, and as you add people to follow you'll start to see some strange stuff in your feed. You'll also see messages that are relevant to your book and writing career. You can reply to these and that can be the start of a conversation on the topic. It will take some time for you to adjust to Twitter and to get comfortable with it.

An important part of Twitter (and many other sites) is hashtags. These are words or phrases preceded by a #. Hashtags are Twitter talk for keywords. You can add one or two hashtags (or more) to your tweet so people interested in that hashtag can find it. If you click on a hashtag in a tweet, you'll see a list of current tweets on that subject.

Some of the hashtags I use are:
#fantasy
#scifi
#humor
#satire
#amwriting
#publishing
#Selfpublishing
#bookmarketing

There are many, many more hashtags you can employ. As you use Twitter, you'll come across more or them and become comfortable using them.

Join LinkedIn

LinkedIn is a site for professionals from all types of businesses including the writing and publishing industries. It's quite different from Facebook. You'll find it at this web location: https://www.linkedin.com

After you sign up, browse the site to gain an understanding of it, then search for writing and publishing groups. There are a lot of them, so be selective. Don't join them all or you'll be overwhelmed with emails. The value of these groups is that you can ask questions and get useful information from the other group members. Most importantly, you can ask for names of editors or cover artists. The names you get will be ones who have been used by the other LinkedIn members and aren't likely to be scam artists.

You can also ask questions on almost any aspect of writing and publishing and you'll get responses. If, as you browse the web, you come across an 'interesting 'marketing offer, ask in the groups if anyone has experience or has interacted with the offerer. The responses may clarify if the offer is legitimate or not.

LinkedIn uses hashtags similar to Twitter.

Other Social Media Sites

There are many more social media sites and you can explore them on your own. Use them or not as you see fit. Perhaps there is a better way to use your time then joining too many social media sites, but that is a personal choice.

Chapter 3: Marketing Content

Introduction

Marketing content is all about developing material that can be used in marketing activities. Much of the copy you generate can be used by itself, some of it will be incorporated with other content to produce additional material.

Here is a list of topics to be covered in this section.

- ☐ Book blurb
- ☐ Book Description
- ☐ Keyword analysis
- ☐ Keyword applications
- ☐ Prequel edition
- ☐ Sig files
- ☐ Sampling
- ☐ Trailer

As you can see, there is a lot of material here.

Book Blurb

The purpose of the book blurb is to grab the attention of a potential reader. Once you have her attention by means of a great pitch line as the opening sentence, you need to follow that up with a few more sentences that tell her what's different about your book and what's in it for her.

Many new authors consider a book blurb to be a short synopsis. This is a mistake. Book blurbs and a short synopsis are two different animals and they have different purposes.

Here are descriptions for each of the three elements involved in developing a book blurb. Some of the material you developed in your strategic marketing plan will be helpful here. Keep the blurb to less than a hundred words if possible and no longer than a hundred-fifty words.

Pitch Line: This is the first statement and it is the hook to grab the reader's attention. Its purpose is to persuade the reader to keep reading the other two statements. It should be simple, one or two sentences at most, and it must make a clear statement about your book.

What's in it for the buyer? This is a statement that explains what the reader (i.e. a book buyer) will get in exchange for money. This must be explicit. This statement is not the place to get cute. Don't come across like the legendary used-car salesman. Tell the reader what benefit he'll get from buying the book. Think of this statement in this way; if your book is surrounded by hundreds of similar-sized books on a shelf in a bookstore, what would persuade the buyer to choose your book instead of one of the others?

What's different about this book? With all the books published every month, what makes your book stand out from the others?

The secret to creating an effective blurb is to keep rewriting and condensing it until it expresses the ideas with a minimum of words.

For example, this is the book blurb for my novel _Falstaff's Big Gamble_.

Pitch Line: _This novel is Shakespeare's Worst Nightmare._

What's in it for the buyers? _It takes two of the Bard's most famous plays, Hamlet and Othello, and recasts them into a fantasy land called Gundarland. There, Hamlet becomes a dwarf and Othello a dark elf_

What's different about this book? _If that isn't bad enough, these two tragedies are now comedies with Falstaff, Shakespeare's most popular rogue, thrown in as a bonus._

For my non-fiction how-to book _Planning a Novel, Script or Memoir,_

I developed this blurb.

Pitch Line: Creating a long story such as a novel requires a great deal of effort and creativity. It is easy to get lost in details and to lose focus on the main issues.

What's in it for the buyers? This book describes a process to plan the work prior to writing the first draft. The purpose of the plan is to allow the author to concentrate on the important elements of the story.

What's different about the book? A major portion of the book describes a method of developing a roadmap to keep the writer on target. The plan can be used to develop any long story such as a novel, a script, a memoir or even a play.

Here is a tongue-in-cheek blurb for a memoir.

Pitch Line: I really only wanted to study math, but I ended up ruling the world.

What's in for the buyers? I reveal my secret to manipulate the markets and gain control of a commodity and possibly the world.

What's different about the book? I tell my story of how, after getting advanced degrees in math and computer science, I dabbled in the stock market and cornered the market for Stanislite, the rare mineral that gives superheroes their unique powers, thus gaining control over the superheroes.

So what are blurbs good for other than what was discussed above? How else can they be used? You can use them anywhere they'll fit. If you can't fit the entire statement someplace (such as on *Twitter*), use the pitch line by itself. You can also use them on websites, in book trailers, in announcements and in press releases.

If you have a publisher check the blurb it created. If yours is stronger send it to the publisher and ask them to replace theirs with yours. It may do so, but at least you asked.

If your self-published book is available, see if your original short description should be replaced by your new blurb.

Book Description:

The book description on Amazon or Barnes & Noble or other book seller web site, is your opportunity to persuade a visitor to buy your book. Perhaps the visitor is just browsing or maybe some marketing content of yours caught their attention. No matter how the visitor arrived at your book page, this visitor has a least a cursory interest in the book. So now the job of the book description is to close the sale.

All the visitor will see is a few lines of copy of your book description. Those few lines must convince the visitor to click on the "Read more" link.

Writing a book description for a fiction book is quite different from a non-fiction book.

For fiction, the description should attempt to get the visitor interested in the main character and that character's problem.

With a non-fiction book, the goal is to convince the visitor that your book will solve a problem the visitor has. After all, if a visitor landed on your book page, that visitor must have at least a passing interest in the problem. So now the visitor sees your description. It consist of four lines of text (on Amazon) and those lines must convince her to click on "Read more." If your description doesn't do that, the visitor will leave the page.

Writing those four lines of text (and what follows) must persuade the visitor to buy the book.

That ain't easy! Fortunately, there is an excellent tutorial on writing a description for a non-fiction book. Here is a link to it: http://authorjourneyto100k.com/6-steps-to-a-perfect-book-description-that-sells-tons-of-books/

Using the tutorial I wrote this description for my book, *Creating Stories*.

You have a story to tell. Let it out!

Imagine developing a story and telling it in a way that will keep the readers turning the pages.

Hank Quense, the author of more than a dozen highly-regarded novels, shows you how to do it.

In the book, you'll learn how to:

* Develop imagery the reader can use

* Build well-rounded characters the readers will relate to

* Create a path through the plot cloud

* Develop an emotional arc to keep readers on the edge of their seats

* Write dramatic and effective scenes

* Employ story-telling techniques to hold the readers' interest

* and much more

Buy this book now and start telling your story.

Pick up your copy today by clicking on the buy now button on the top of the page.

Keyword Analysis

Keywords are frequently referred to as tags.

Readers will often search for a book using the name of a best-selling author but readers can't enter your title or name since you and your book have achieved little recognition. So far!

Another way readers will search for a book is by using a short descriptive phrase such as 'fantasy quest 'or 'regency romance'. This is the situation where you want your book to appear in the search results. To accomplish this, it is vital that you develop a set of keywords that will ensure your book title will show up in the reader's search results.

The keywords you want to use are ones that readers in your genre will use when browsing for a book. These keywords are not necessarily what your book is about: they are the terms a reader will type into a search engine. Let's say your book is a fantasy novel filled with elves and dwarfs. You may think 'dwarfs 'and 'elves 'would be great keywords. They are not. A reader looking for a fantasy novel won't use them, but instead will search on keywords like 'fantasy adventure 'or 'fantasy quest.' Consequently, it is important for your marketing efforts that you develop a relevant set of keywords.

Google has a free keyword planner you can use to help generate your keywords. You can access it using this link: https://ads.google.com/home/tools/keyword-planner/

Another free keyword tool can be found here: https://keywordtool.io/

If you have a publisher, it will generate your keywords. If you self-published your book, check if the keywords should be updated.

Keyword Applications

Keywords are powerful marketing tools. Besides the uses mentioned in the Keyword Analysis, there are other applications.

By now, you probably have written both a long and short synopsis and a blurb. Well now that you have a set of keywords, it's time to update the synopses and the blurb to incorporate the keywords. Why? Because search engines love this usage.

As an example of how this works, here is the blurb for my novel _The King Who Disappeared_ before I generated the keywords: _'A long time ago, Bohan was a king. But that was before the sleep spell. Now that he's awake again, it's time for revenge. '_

The keywords I used are: fantasy adventure, fantasy quest, fantasy humor, fantasy comedy .

Using these keywords, I modified the book blurb to: _'A long time ago, at the beginning of this <u>fantasy adventure</u>, Bohan was a king._

But that was before the sleep spell. Now that he's awake again, it's time for a <u>quest</u> to get revenge. <u>Fantasy humor</u> doesn't get better than this.'

Do you get the idea? Now spend some time and modify the long and short synopses.   Pepper the blurb and synopsis with your keywords. Don't force it, however. Insert them only when it fells natural.

Prequel Edition

It you are self-publishing the book and it isn't available yet, consider this marketing tactic. Before you upload it, make a separate ebook edition consisting of the book's forward and first two chapters. Have a new cover made adding the word Sampler or Prequel to it. (Most cover artist will do this for a nominal charge or they may even do it for free.)

Once you have this sampler ready, upload it and make it available for free. This should be done at least a month before the launch date of the complete book. The point of this activity is to get as many readers as possible to grab a copy of the prequel. If they are impressed by it, they will anticipate the availability of the complete book.

If you used Smashwords as the packager for the prequel, you can price it as a freebie. If your packager is Kindle, you will have to price it at $.99 which defeats the purpose of having a free prequel. Put it on your website as a free download.

Now tell the world about it. You can attach it to emails, you can tweet about it. Generally try to give away as many copies as possible before the launch date.

This works well for both fiction and non-fiction books.

The more different formats you have for the prequel, the better.

Both pdf and epub version of the ebook are easy to make. Getting a mobi version (for Kindle tablets) will be a bit harder. You will have to use a conversion service and the results may be unpredictable.

Here is the Prequel cover for my book *How to Self-publish and Market a Book.* I made it available about a month before the book was released and gave away as many copies as possible.

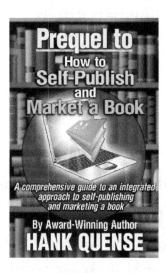

Signature Files

Now is a good time for you to develop a sig file. Email signatures (usually called sig files) are a free way to publicize your book every time you send out an email. Think about how many times a day that happens!

Sig files are those links you see beneath the name of the person who sent you the email. Here is what yours could look like:

Your name

Title of your book

Location of your website

The last two lines would be linked to a webpage, the first to a book buying page like Amazon, the second to your blog page.

Sig files are easy to implement and only take a few minutes. For the Mac mail program, open mail, click on preferences and then on signatures. This will open a new screen like the one shown below.

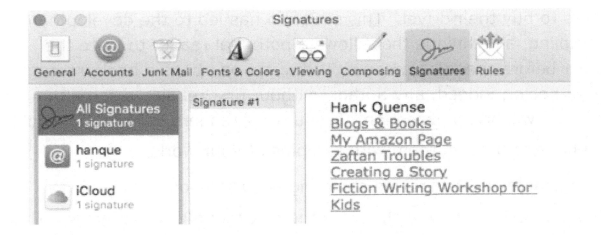

On the left is a list of your email accounts (if you have more than one). The middle column lists the signatures you have established. Right now, it's probably blank. Click on the (+) button and type a file name, such as 'sig 1'. In the right column, you can add the sig files you want and they will be linked to the sig name. To do this, type the name of your book in the right column, highlight the book name, right click on the mouse and click on 'link 'and then type or paste the URL of your book page. Close the screen and every time you send out a new email, the link to your book's page will go with it.

With Gmail, go to the settings page and scroll down to Signature. There you'll see a text box to add whatever you want appended to your signature. You can add links as you need them. Other email programs will have a similar process to build a sig file.

If you use Outlook, this link will provide information about sig files in that program: https://www.mail-signatures.com/articles/outlook-email-signature-location-and-backup/

Sampling

One of the ripple effects of the new world in publishing is that many of the books now available are pure garbage. People who don't know how to create or write a story nevertheless do exactly that and expect readers to buy their drivel. This situation has led to the development of sampling, a technique that allows a potential reader to taste the product before spending money. Today, no one buys a book from a new author or, indeed, any author, without first reading a sample. Your book will be no exception. If you want readers to buy your book, you'll have to provide them with samples of your work.

One simple way to provide sampling is on the book's Amazon webpage. Make sure you check off the box that allows sampling. This puts an arrow near the cover icon that reads, 'Click to look inside.' It's a sample, in other words.

When you upload a book to Smashwords, you'll come across a box labeled, "Allow Sampling." Check it off and then you'll be asked to specify a percentage of the book to sample. If you check off 10%, what the sampler will see is mostly the front matter stuff and sadly little of the book's text. I recommend allowing at least 20% as the sample size. Other packagers will provide a similar option.

Trailers

Trailers are short movie-like films about your book. They are designed to educate, entice and entertain viewers. When you watch TV, you are constantly bombarded by trailers for movies and TV shows, so you have definitely seen trailers; you can't escape them.

If your marketing budget has funding for a trailer, it is best if you can get it before the launch date and use it in your pre-launch marketing.

Trailers can be expensive if you hire a top-notch production company to put one together for your book. Think $1,000 or more. With advances in software and competition, many production companies now make trailers for a modest fee, generally less than $100. These less expensive trailers can be just as effective as the more expensive ones. You can do a web search to find trailer production companies, but you can also ask on LinkedIn and Goodreads.

You can make a trailer yourself. I do. Granted, my trailers aren't as classy as the ones put out by an expensive production company, but mine get the book's message out.

If you make or commission a trailer, put it on your webpage as well as YouTube and Vimeo and add a link to it in your blog posts. You can also add the YouTube trailer link in tweets. Add the trailer link into your sig files if you wish. Make sure you add it to your Amazon Central page.

If you have a publisher and it didn't make a trailer, tell it about your trailer and ask it to add a link on the book's web page.

If your self-published book is currently available, see if the packager has an option to add the trailer to its information about your book.

Chapter 4: Marketing Activities

Introduction

There are a few items to consider under this heading. They are shown in the list:

- ☐ Author squibs
- ☐ Contact emails
- ☐ Contact bloggers
- ☐ Organize a launch party
- ☐ Blog posts
- ☐ Connect with other authors
- ☐ Wattpad content
- ☐ Social media activities

In practice, your marketing activities are attempts to convince people to buy your book. Before potential readers can decide to buy a book, they must know about the book. So the objective of your marketing activities is to inform readers that the book exists and then get them interested in the content. It is a mistake to plead with readers to buy the book without first getting them interested. On the web, especially with sites like Facebook, you'll find author groups with dozens of posts every day that essentially read, "Buy my book! Please?" Each post consists of the plea, a book cover and often a detail synopsis that goes on and on with seemingly no end. The audience for these messages are other authors who are also writing buy-my-book posts. If you are tempted to post on these groups don't use a synopsis: use the book blurb. One rationalization to use these groups is that they are free. All you invest is time but wasted time to be sure.

Get Author Squibs

While you wrote and prepared your book, you probably came into contact with other authors. If so, you can email them a package of material to tell them about your book and ask them to write a sentence or two praising the book. These are called author squibs. If the other author obliges with a squib, put it on the back cover if you have a print book and in the beginning of the sample material for an ebook.

Some people consider this to be false advertising since the one who wrote the squib probably didn't read the book. However, traditional publishing houses use author squibs extensively. Consider this just one more decision the author has to make.

To squib or not to squib? That is the question.

Contact emails

Here is a free marketing task you can easily take advantage of. You probably have a sizable list of email contacts consisting of family, friends and virtual friends. Tell them about your book. Include the book blurb, the cover image and buy links. Ask them to forward the email to their contacts. Some may do this and that will greatly expand the reach of your marketing activities.

This isn't the only marketing task involving emails. Now that you're a published author, it's time to build another emails list besides the one mentioned above. This one is more professionally oriented and consist of readers who have shown an interest in your books or in your blog posts or your articles. You can maintain connect with these readers by sending out newsletters and updates on your newest book project.

To manage my email lists, (I have several) I use Mailchimp:

www://mailchimp.com. It enables you to put together professional looking emails and newsletters. It will also give you amazing stats such as who opened the email and how many recipients clicked on links in the newsletter. Mailchimp has a free version and a paid version. I haven't seen the need to upgrade to the paid version and I doubt you will need it also.

So how do you go about building an email list? Here is excellent article by a top-notch book marketer: https://www.janefriedman.com/email-newsletter-growth/

Here is another good article, this one by Mailchimp. It discusses adding a signup form to capture important contact data for your list: https://mailchimp.com/help/add-a-signup-form-to-your-website/

Spend time managing your list and remove anyone who requests it. Not removing those names means you'll be spamming them with future emails.

Contact Bloggers

As your social media's presence expands, you will come in contact with bloggers. These are valuable contacts, especially the ones who review books and publish articles from guests. Make a note of these bloggers and their web sites.

Once your book is almost available, send them a note asking if they are interested in reviewing your book. In your note, send them the book blurb and a cover image. Do not send out a query for a romance book to a site that reviews fantasy books. You're wasting your time and the bloggers time in doing this.

If you ask for a review and don't get a reply right away, don't bug the reviewer. Review bloggers are overwhelmed with requests and it takes time for them to weed through all the requests. You should be aware that the bloggers only review a small number of requests. It helps if they know your name, especially if they know your name because you had a guest post on their site.

If a blogger accepts your request for a review, make sure you visit the website occasional and post comments if appropriate. Small activities like these will make the blogger more open to your future requests.

Organize a Launch Team

Let's begin with a definition of a street team: *A street team is a dedicated group of readers who like your work and are interested in helping promote your books. These readers are interested in helping to promote your book because your relationship with them is mutually beneficial*: Writers Digest

Recruiting a street team provides multiple benefits. One of these is readers to help you promote your book. Image: your street team forwards your book information to their contacts. This multiples your social media reach immensely and would be almost impossible to achieve on your own.

Rather than duplicate detailed information readily found on the web, I'll provide a few links that will describe how to recruit a team and how use it.

https://www.iuniverse.com/en/resources/book-marketing-and-self-promotion/6-steps-to-build-a-street-team-and-promote-your-book

https://www.writersdigest.com/publishing-insights/develop-street-team-book

https://blog.reedsy.com/authors-build-your-street-team-4-simple-steps/

https://bookmarketingtools.com/blog/22-ways-to-leverage-your-street-team-for-a-book-launch/

Blog Posts

Blog posts are most effective when used just prior to launch and afterwards. They're free and only require your labor and creativity and they can be written in advance. Fiction and non-fiction books have quite different criteria for the blog posts. Non-fiction books lend themselves to blog posts more readily than fiction books.

All blog posts about your book must include the cover image and buy links. Otherwise, the work involved is wasted. With a buy link, the reader may be tempted to click on the link and could buy the book. Without a buy link, the visitor has no way to easily find the book and the visitor will rarely, if ever, be intrigued enough to start a web search to find it.

With non-fiction books, you can write blog posts about any topic in the book and any related topic, even if the connection is a bit obscure. Is your book about plumbing repairs? Write articles on the different types of pipes available: copper, plastic, iron with the advantages and disadvantages of each. Another article can explain the different types of faucets.

With fiction books you have to be more creative. Possible posts could contain a scene or two. Or a related short story. I like to develop tongue-in-cheek interviews with my characters.

Once you have the post on your website or someone else's, tell the world about. Put the link and a description on Facebook, Twitter and other social media sites. You want to drive people to read the post.

Connect With Other Authors

Your list of author contacts is valuable information. When your book is in pre-launch or after it becomes available, ask your author friends to spread the word about it. If they tell their contacts where your book can be ordered, it will do wonders for your social media reach. Of course, you should tell them that you will reciprocate when their next book is available,.

Many of your author friends also have blogs. Perhaps they'll let you be a guest and post a review about your book. Or perhaps they can interview you and ask questions about the book.

Since the other authors may be too busy to make up a list of questions, send them a list you made up and let them pick a half-dozen for your interview. This saves them time and you can slant the questions to discuss whatever issues you want to discuss and to emphasize the points you want to make.

Wattpad content

Wattpad is a site you can use to let people read part of your book. You can find the website here: https://www.wattpad.com

Once you establish an account, you can post material that others can find, read, rate and post comments about. If the reader likes what she read she may tell others about the content and these others will visit your post. Typical material can include an entire chapter, a scene or two or even an entire section of the book.

A word about your copyrights: before you can post a story on Wattpad, you have to create an account and log in. Only other logged in members can read your story. In other words, it is not available to general public. Since the only way to access the story is through the website that is secured by a password and login procedure, it is not considered 'published'.

To clarify what this means, your story is still considered unpublished even though dozens of Wattpad members read it. You can still sell the first rights to the story.

Social Media Activity

When the book launch approaches, it's a good time to increase your social media presence. One effective way to do this is to become active in groups dedicated to writing and reading. Facebook, LinkedIn and Goodreads all have such groups. You can also explore other social media sites such as Pinterest, Reddit, Instagram and others. Join them if they seem right for you.

Here are a few groups you can join on Goodreads:

Indie and Self-published Author Support:
https://www.goodreads.com/group/show/154447-support-for-indie-authors

Authors and Reviewers:
https://www.goodreads.com/group/show/103713-authors-reviewers

Support for Indie Authors:
https://www.goodreads.com/group/show/103713-authors-reviewers

Advanced Copies for Review and Book Giveaways:
https://www.goodreads.com/group/show/58575-advanced-copies-for-review-book-giveaways

With LinkedIn, potential groups to join include:
New Authors Need Marketing Ideas:
https://www.linkedin.com/groups/1725677/

Book Marketing Tips: https://www.linkedin.com/groups/1848415/

Self-published and Indie Authors Networking Group:
https://www.linkedin.com/groups/2826012/

Book Story: https://www.linkedin.com/groups/5148410/

Facebook also has a number of groups for authors. My experience with those groups is they tend to be an endless array of 'buy my book' posts and I dropped out of them. There may be more suitable groups to search for. How you go about increasing your web presence is a personal choice. However, I can offer a few words of advice.

Don't start arguments. You won't win them, not on the web anyway. All you'll do is annoy some of your contacts. And I would advise you to ignore arguments others have started, even if you have an opinion and an urge to jump in. On the other hand, don't be too bland. A little controversy can go a long way.

What you want to do in the groups is reply to questions and to join discussions on topics you feel you're qualified to talk about.

Don't pimp your book in the groups, even if others are doing exactly that. Reserve book marketing tweets and posts for non-group activities.

Chapter 5: Book Reviews

Book reviews are probably the most potent of all marketing activities. There is no such thing as having too many reviews. What's great about a good review is that it tells potential buyers that someone else read and liked the book. A good book review is a powerful marketing tool. You can use it by positioning it on your blog. You can also share it by using the social media links.

The content in this chapter is listed here:

- ☐ Advance review copies
- ☐ Previous reviewers
- ☐ Friends and family
- ☐ Social media requests
- ☐ Book Review Buzz
- ☐ Goodreads reviews
- ☐ Kindle Review Service
- ☐ Librarything reviews
- ☐ Reader's Favorite
- ☐ Booksprout
- ☐ Netgalley
- ☐ Reedsy
- ☐ Self-publishing Reviews

I have heard (but haven't experienced) that Amazon helps you advertise your book if the book gets 50 or more reviews. Trust me, that ain't easy to do, but it is a great goal to have.

There are several strategies you can use to acquire more reviews. Goodreads groups are a fertile area to request reviews. Use these groups as your first recourse. A few such groups are listed later in this chapter.

Another approach is to contact a review site. These come in two flavors. One will review your book, usually for a fee. Self-publishing Reviews is such a site. So is Booklife. Some sites will review your book for free. Reader's Favorite is one although it will prompt you to upgrade to a paid review.

The second type of review site won't actually review your book, but will make it available to a number of potential reviewers. I list a few of these later in the chapter. There are many more besides the ones I mention, but I only included ones I'm familiar with. A simple search will give you a list of more sites offering to get book reviews in return for a price.

Let me be clear: if you use one of these services, you are not *buying* a review like you would with the Self-publishing Review site. You're paying for a review service that will put your book in front of many potential reviewers who may or may not elect to review your book. Reviewers who chose to read your book are not paid by the review service. What you are paying for when you sign up for a review service is access to all the potential reviewers on its list.

Some of the review services will not deliver the goods. They talk a good story about the many reviewers they have on their email list, but you won't get the number of reviews you signed up for. These sites simply don't have enough readers on their list to deliver the reviews. Others, a small number, are just scammers looking to rip off authors.

Another strategy is to give away copies of your book, hopefully in exchange for a promise to review it. You can use your social media contacts here. Ask if anyone wants a free ebook review copy. I've found this tactic to be marginally effective. The main reason is that some people ask for a review copy only because it's free and they have no intention of ever writing a review. Also some readers won't like the book and won't write a negative review. My experience is that between 25% to 50% of these readers will write a review. However, ebooks don't cost you anything to send to potential reviewers so you aren't incurring any costs.

Some readers might be reluctant to write a review because they aren't sure how to go about doing it. You can help them out by sending along a list of questions that will assist those people in putting together a review. I have lists of questions at the end of this chapter. There are two lists: one for fiction and one for non-fiction.

There are also reputable sites you can use to get prestigious reviews, such as Kirkus Reviews. You can find it here: Kirkusreviews.com. This is a site that will review your book, but it requires a large fee ($425 at this writing). Once you pay, you will get a review and you'll see it before it's published. You can then decide if you want it to go public or not. This prevents a stinker of a review from seeing the light of day. If you agree to let it go public, the review will appear on the website and will attract attention. A Kirkus review also looks great on Amazon and other seller websites. Since you paid for it, Amazon does not allow the review to be posted against your book like all the other reviews. However, you can add it to the book on your Amazon Central page under "editorial reviews."

Booklife is part of Publishers Weekly https://booklife.com. It offers a review service. It is expensive ($399 right now) but it provides a detailed review of the book in several categories. .

There are many more review sites than the ones listed in this section. I only listed ones I'm familiar with. To find others, you'll have to do a web search. But be careful! Read all the fine print before committing to use a review site.

Advanced Review copies

Advanced Review Copies (or ARCs) are a great boon to getting early reviews besides being an opportunity to catch a few additional typos. Once you get ARCs, you can offer them to book reviewers to read before the book becomes available. Getting them is a bit tricky depending upon who your ebook packager is. If you use Smashwords to package and distribute your ebook, you can download an ebook in epub or other format at any time. You are then free to give out copies of these as you see fit.

If your packager is Kindle, the situation is quite different. You can only get a mobi formatted ebook and that is tricky to get.

When you upload the file to Kindle, at some point in the process, you will be asked if you wish to review the ebook file on your computer. Answer yes and Kindle will send a mobi edition to your computer for your review. You can get another copy if you wish by going to your Kindle dashboard and selecting "edit ebook content". This option will allow you to download another copy of the book.

If Kindle is your only packager, then having only a mobi version limits your ability to engage with reviewers who need an epub or pdf edition. You can develop your own pdf edition by exporting your master file.

There are websites that offer to convert a mobi edition to other formats such as epub. The sites offer the reverse also: epub to mobi. Many of theses sites will require an account to use it and some require a subscription. One site you can use free is https://www.zamzar.com.

With print books, you'll be required to order one and review it before it will be become available for sale. You will then have to approve it or send a revised manuscript. Unlike ebooks, you will be charged production and mailing costs for the ARC. However, if you are confident the book is in good shape, you can order more than a single copy. These then become your Advanced Review Copies.

Friends and Family

Your list of contacts and friends are a good source of potential reviewers. If you contacted them about the book when it was published, now is a good time to contact them again and ask if they are interested in reviewing it. If so, send them a complementary copy of the ebook.

You can also ask them to forward your email and the review request to their contact list.

Social Media Requests

You can use your social media accounts to ask for reviews. Simply post the book blurb and the cover and ask if anyone would like a review copy. The main issue here is that most of the responses will come from total strangers. You literally do not know who you are sending a copy of the book to. It might be a pirate site for all you know. If it is, your book will end up on a site which is selling it and not paying you royalties. This is remote possibility, however.

Some other responders will simply ask for the review copy with no intention of ever writing a review. That's life.

Book Review Buzz

http://bookreviewbuzz.com is a book review site. For a small fee, the site will add your book and promote it to their contacts who may or may not chose to review the book. The site sends out a weekly newsletter with new books available to review.

Like almost all book review sites, this one deals only with ebooks, not print books.

The site has several price options for reviews. In the least expensive, you provide the reviewers with a copy of the book. The site will provide the book copy for a higher service fee. They also have an expensive option in which your book will appear on the NetGalley site.

The site offers book publishing services. Actually, what the site does is transfer you to a publisher. With all links like this, be careful you don't fall into the clutches of a vanity press. You should use caution and do a web search before approaching this or any publisher.

Goodreads Review Groups

One great feature about Goodreads is that there are millions of readers on it. And those readers love to get free books to read and review. There are a number of groups that actively seek authors looking for reviews.

One such group is called Advanced Copies for Review & Book Giveaways. Here is a link to it: https://www.goodreads.com/group/show/58575-advanced-copies-for-review-book-giveaways

A second group is: Authors and Reviewers: https://www.goodreads.com/group/show/103713-authors-reviewers

There are more such groups on Goodreads, but these are the two that I have used to get book reviews.

When you request a review (your book must be on Goodreads), use your book blurb. You can also use your short synopsis. If group members are interested in your book, they will leave a message for you.

Browse these groups and read the review requests. If you see a book that sounds interesting, request a copy. Interactions like this increase your exposure within the group.

At one time, Goodreads had a great service in which an author could give away a certain number of copies of an ebook. So you could set up a give away offer for say 10 copies and Goodreads would run the promotion and collect names of members who applied for he book. It was a raffle. After the raffle completed, Goodreads randomly selected the winners and sent you an email with the names.

Then Amazon bought Goodreads and the free giveaway suddenly turned into an expensive giveaway. Currently there are two offerings to give away 100 copies of the ebook. One costs $119 and the second $599.

Services like this are called ripoffs for good reason. That's my personal opinion. However, for a different perspective, here is what author Elizabeth Craig says:

What is your favorite or most successful marketing tactic?

My favorite and I feel most-successful marketing tactic is the Goodreads Giveaway. I do the $119 one.

How do you use it?

I use the giveaway to add awareness of and visibility for my series. If I have a new release coming up, I'll run a giveaway for the first book of the series. The giveaway is for as many as 100 ebooks, although you can give away as few as 10. Goodreads handles everything: they notify the winners and distribute the ebooks. I pay for the giveaway through my Amazon account. The coolest thing is that everyone who enters the giveaway has my book added to their "want to read" list, which also shows up in their friends' feeds on the site.

So there you have it: once again, you face a decision. To buy a giveaway or not.

Kindle Review Service

This is a review site that restricts its service to books that are available through Kindle You can find it here:
https://www.ireviewkindlebooks.com/amazon-services/

Despite the name, the site is not part of Amazon or Kindle, but they are an Amazon affiliate and receive compensation on Amazon purchases made through the site.

The site will review your book either before or after the publication date. It charges a fee to review the book. The site also offers other services such as a book assessment. Naturally these extra services have additional fees.

Apparently, you won't find out the price until after you submit the book for review.

Librarything

This is a site that has many similarities to Goodreads. It is also quite different. It's much smaller than Goodreads. You can find the website here: https://www.librarything.com

Once you sign up and identify yourself as an author, you can put your books on the site and request reviews.

Reader's Favorite

Yet another review site: https://readersfavorite.com

You can send them a copy of your book and request a free review. The book will be shown to their extensive list of reviewers who select what books they want to review. A free review, if selected by a reviewer, will take up to eight weeks or more. After a few months you may get an email saying that no one wanted to review it.

The site also offers guaranteed reviews for a fee. That means all reviews from this site can't be posted on Amazon like most reviews are. This applies whether you received a free review or if you paid for it. You can however add it to your Amazon Central page where it will show up under editorial reviews.

Reader's Favorite also runs a large contest once a year.

Booksprout

This one is a free review site. https://booksprout.co. Once you have an account, you can upload your book and request reviews. You can do this before or after the book is launched. The site will allow up to twenty readers to request a copy. That doesn't imply your book will get that many requests. You may only receive a handful of requests and not all of the them will post a review. Still, you'll get a few

reviews. A neat feature of this site is that the reviews won't just show up on Amazon. They will also appear on Goodreads and other book sellers such as Barnes & Noble.

NetGalley

Part of Smith Publicity, it is a vast site used by publishers to solicit readers and reviewers to take a look at advanced review copies of the book. You can find it here: https://www.netgalley.com

NetGalley is used by many traditional publishers and small indie press houses. There is a cost to offering a book for review but the results may be worth the expense

Reedsy

This is another site that will submit your book to a large list of reviewers in return for a fee. You can find the website here: https://reedsy.com/discovery

The site specializes in books that aren't yet launched or were

recently launched. As such, getting a good review here can supplement your launch promotions.

Self-publishing Reviews

This is a sprawling site with many options including a link to get your book published from what appears to be a vanity press. Editing and other pre-publishing services are offered. The site will review your book and it has several levels of reviews coupled with promotions. The reviews start at $89 at this time.

Go to https://www.selfpublishingreview.com/get-reviewed to learn more.

Book Review Questionnaires

It's my observation that many people don't write reviews for books they enjoy because they aren't sure how to go about writing one. To alleviate this problem I wrote up a series of questions to help readers compose a short, simple book review. There are two versions of this: one for fiction and one for nonfiction.   When asking someone to review your book or when sending along an ebook copy for review, paste the questions into the email or you can create a document and attach it to the email.

Fiction Book Review Questionnaire:

On a scale of 1 to 5 (5 being the highest) how would rate this book?

1) Did you like or dislike the book?

2) Please explain why you answered 2) as you did.

If you liked the book, please answer the following questions:

3) Why did you like the book?

4) What didn't you like about the book?

5) Did the main characters seem real and believable to you?

6) Did you want the book to continue beyond the ending?

Use your answers to these questions to write a few sentences about the book. Hint: don't write a brief synopsis.

Non-fiction Book Review Questionnaire:

How many stars, from 1 to 5 would you give this book? (Five is the highest rating)

1) What did you like about the book (if anything)?

2) What didn't you like about the book (if anything)?

3) Did you get the information the author promised in the book

blurb and other promotional material?

4) Did the book contain information you weren't expected or didn't know about?

5) Would you recommend this book to others?

Use your answers to these questions to write a few sentences about the book.

Chapter 6: Events

Introduction

Events are a potentially great way to increase exposure and sales. The events discussed here require a lot of work in preparation for the happening. Some events may also require funding.

Topics to be explored in this chapter include:

- ☐ Physical launch party
- ☐ Webinars
- ☐ Twitter chats
- ☐ Video chats
- ☐ Online launch party
- ☐ Book giveaways
- ☐ Physical book events

These activities will be problematic for many authors because events are quite different from the other marketing tactics. Many of the events will require personal appearances and public speaking. This can be a traumatic experience for first time authors if the author is:

1) shy or introverted.

2) not accustomed to public speaking.

For those authors, I can offer some advice. Never forget, you are the expert on the book you are speaking about. No one in the room knows as much as you do. No matter how nervous you are, talk and act like an expert and you have a great chance of getting through the event. You may even learn that you enjoyed the experience.

*Physical Launch Part*y

A physical launch party is usually held for print books since the

main purpose is to sell copies of the book.
https://blog.bookbaby.com/2018/10/10-tips-for-hosting-a-successful-book-launch-party/ has a number of tips on hosting such a party.

The date of the party is selected to coincide with the book's availability date. This requires a bit of advanced planning and organization. For instance, prior to the date, you will have to order a supply of books to sell at the event. Since this is a 'party, 'it is customary to have refreshments at the event. This could be pastries and soda or wine and cheese.

In the case of traditionally published books, the launch party is usually held in a book store and is organized by the publisher. If your book is self-published, you will have to do this. Probably, local books stores won't be interested in hosting your party unless you have name recognition from some other activity such as being a war hero, a famous politician, a notorious felon and so forth. Without the claim to fame, the book store will rightfully conclude you won't attract a crowd and hence, it won't agree to allow you to hold the event in the store.

In this case, the next best thing is to hold it in a local library. Libraries are more open than book stores to allowing self-publishing authors to hold such events. The library will also promote the event in their newsletters or email announcements.

Once the event starts, the author becomes the focus of everyone's attention. This can be traumatic for shy authors who aren't used to speaking in public. In the case of a novel, the event usually consists of the author reading scenes from the books. Personally, I hate to read scenes aloud! I find it boring to me and to the audience. I prefer to talk about the novel's background and the main characters. Non-fiction books are a lot easier to talk about than a novel. Presumably, the non-fiction book addresses a problem unless it is a memoir or a biography. If it addresses a problem the author can talk about the problem and how the book solves the problem.

After the reading, the audience — in theory — lines up to throw money at the author in return for a signed copy of the book. This may or may not happen. Being an author is a tough job.

Webinars

If you have a non-fiction book other than a memoir or a biography, you can hold a webinar. Rather than simply pitching the book, you provide information or a demonstration about solving a problem, a problem that is addressed in the book. To use the example of a book about plumbing repairs, the webinar could explain how to repair a leaky faucet.

To host a webinar you will require an online software program that allows you to share the screen. This will permit you to show slides or videos to your audience. Without this screen sharing capability, the webinar will consist only of your mugshot and whatever you can hold up in your hands.

One webinar site is: https://www.eztalks.com

Besides the software, you will have to promote the webinar in order to attract an audience. Your social media accounts will be useful for this purpose. In your posts, you will have to announce the time and a URL link.

At the conclusion of the event, show a copy of your book, either physical or virtual and provide buy-links where the audience can grab a copy. You can also offer a deal for a limited time discounted offer.

With a memoir, the webinar is about the person in the book, you. If you're not famous or notorious, the webinar will have a limited appeal may people. The same is true about a biography.

Hosting a webinar for a novel is different and difficult for the same reasons mentioned under the launch party section.

Twitter Chats

Twitter chats are a unique way to engage with others on the social media platform. A chat can be organized around almost any topic but it should have some connection with the book you are selling.

There is a lot of material on the web about how to organize a Twitter chat so I won't repeat it here. You can visit this website to learn how to do it and to see if this type of event is something you want to do: https://blog.hootsuite.com/a-step-by-step-guide-to-twitter-chats/

Video Chats

A video chat is similar to a webinar but is less formal and is more suitable for a novel. You'll need a chat software application such as Zoom, Google Hangout, Facebook Live or a different one. You'll also need a promotional plan to spread the word about the event.

During the event, you can talk to the audience similar to what you would do for a launch party. You can also have a question and answer session.

As with webinars, show a copy of your book at the end, either physical of virtual and provide buy-links where the audience can grab a copy. You can also offer a deal for a limited time discounted offer.

Online Launch Party

If your book is an ebook only, you can choose to hold an online launch party. This is similar to a webinar or a video chat, except it is held to celebrate the ebook's availability. Instead of providing refreshments, you can offer gifts such as a free copy of the book, or some swag you ordered in advanced. The swag could include keychains, coffee mugs and so forth. This of course will involve postage costs. One way to implement this part of the party is to use Etsy to buy and ship the swag. WWW.etsy.com.

The launch party will have to be organized in advance and you'll have to promote the event on social media including the party's URL.

Here is a link to an article on virtual launch parties: https://authorunlimited.com/blog/virtual-book-launch.

Here's a link with creative ideas for the launch party: https://www.peerspace.com/resources/creative-book-launch-ideas.

Book Giveaways

One way to gain readers is to give away copies of your book. Giveaways are different from running an ad promoting a book that is free. Giveaways are much more targeted.

There are a number of reasons to run a giveaway. First, some of these readers may post a review. Second, the giveaway may enable you to grow your list of emails. Third, it increases your name recognition. Finally, it can lead to future sales.

If you give away a print book, you'll incur both production and postage costs in getting the books from the packager, and then you'll have more postage costs when you send it out. If you give away an ebook, it doesn't cost you anything. Ebooks don't have production costs and they don't have postage requirements. However, print book giveaways will attract more interest; especially if you sign the book with the reader's name.

Here are a few ways you can give away the book.

You can write a blog post stating that you're giving away X copies of your new book in a random drawing to people who sign up via an email form. You can use Mailchimp for this effort. Mailchimp has a simple email signup form you can use and you'll get a notice every time someone fills out the form. At the end of the signup period, select the winners and attach the ebook to an email. Ask the winners to write a review if they enjoy the book. Spread the word about your giveaway on Twitter, Facebook, LinkedIn and wherever else you have accounts.

You can commission an online raffle using a site like Rafflecopter: https://www.rafflecopter.com. This site has a paid monthly subscription plan. Sign up for it if you plan to run a lot of raffles, otherwise use its free trial offer. Use your social media accounts to promote the raffle.

If you have your book on Smashwords, you can change the price of the book to a free download and run this sale for a limited period of time. Promote the freebie using social media.

If you have your book on Kindle and it's enrolled it in Kindle Select you can offer your book for free five days in every quarter. Promote the offer using social media.

The disadvantage of using Smashwords and Kindle as the way to give away your book is you don't know who downloaded it. In this case, your chances of gaining reviews are next to nothing. A reason for this is the capacity of tablets. It is virtually unlimited. Readers can (and many do) download every interesting free book they come across. They may read your book some day, but that day could be far into the future. In other words, the benefits of this book giveaway are marginal at best.

Another tactic many authors use is to permanently list their book as a free download. I don't believe this action has any benefits. An author should want to sell his book, not give it away forever. Running an occasional giveaway has some benefits to the author. Offering a permanent free download has few, if any, benefits.

Physical Book Events

Ebooks are sold almost exclusively on the internet. Print books are sold via the web, in bookstores and at events you attend or organize. Libraries are another potential market for print books.

Book stores

Book stores are a tough nut to crack for self-published authors, especially if it's a first book and the author has no name recognition.

Most book stores in this country use Ingram as their distributor. If your book is distributed by Ingram, is returnable and has the industry standard discount (55%) there is a chance book stores will order your book and put it on their shelves for a while. However, book stores will not know about the book's existence unless you tell them about it.

Contacting book stores one at a time is a mind-numbing activity, especially if you pursue out-of-area and out-of-state book stores. The only cost-effective way to query these stores is by using email.

Just because your book isn't on a shelf in a book store doesn't mean the store can't order a copy if a customer requests one. Barnes & Noble and other book stores can order a print copy of the book just by entering the ISBN number or the book title into their computer system. Within a few days, the book will arrive ready to be picked up by the customer who ordered it.

If your print book packager is Kindle, there is no, nada, zippo, zilch, not-a-prayer of the book store ordering a copy of the book to put on its shelves. Kindle will not allow returns, and that is a deal breaker as far as the book store is concerned. Although the book store won't put the Kindle book on its shelves, it can and will order a copy if a customer requests it.

Assuming you get books into a book store, does that mean the store will arrange a book signing or a launch party for you? Probably not. If you're an unknown author, the book store owner may feel he is wasting his time because few people will come in to see and hear an author they never heard of.

Libraries

Most libraries rely primarily on Baker & Taylor as their distributor, but they will also use Ingram. If your book isn't distributed by one of these two companies, you have very little chance of getting the book onto library shelves unless you give them a free copy.

Once you get the book into a library (start with your local ones), ask if they will arrange a book reading and signing. A library may be more receptive to the signing than a book store will be. They'll usually put a blurb into the local paper, thus increasing your exposure. Make sure you have a supply of books to sell. This should be a budget item that you fund if you have a print edition of your book.

Some libraries may want a slice of revenue if they allow you to sell books at the reading. My experience is they'll want ten percent of whatever you make. I think it's a great deal. Libraries need all the financial help they can get.

Consignments

Consignment selling means the book store (or the local drug store) will take copies of the book, but the store will not order them. They will only accept copies of the book that you order and pay for. This relieves the book store from initially paying for the books and handling returns later on. In other words, it improves their cashflow and transfers inventory management to the author.

Under consignment deals, the book store will keep a percentage of all book sales and the author gets what's left. Typically, the book store will want 25% to 40% of the sale revenue.

A consignment deal typically will last three to six months. At the end of the period, you settle the payment issue and walk away with the unsold books under your arm and a check in your pocket. If some books were sold, the book store may agree to renew the deal.

Consignment selling requires a contract that is signed by the author and the store. The contract will contain the book title, number of books in the deal, the book price and the store's percentage of sales.

You can find blank contracts at a number of websites including Legalzoom: https://www.legalzoom.com and Rocketlawyer: https://www.rocketlawyer.com

There is one thing to keep in mind with consignment deals: ask whether your book will be displayed on a shelf or dumped in the storage room where no one will ever see them. If your books are slated to go into storage, you may want to rethink the consignment deal.

Book Events

Book events are gatherings such as book fairs where readers go to peruse tables staffed by authors and loaded with their books. These are often run by libraries, at least around where I live.

Other book events are street fairs and flea markets. In these you may have to rent a table from the event's organizers. That means for you to make a profit on the event, you first have to sell enough books to cover the cost of the table.

Chapter 7: Publicity

Introduction

Publicity is another marketing activity you can engage in. Its results in terms of book sales are difficult to quantify. Publicity may lead to book sales, but its real purpose is to spread the word about you and your book.

Here is a quote from a public relations firm: *"One of the biggest advantages of publicity is that it can massively improve your brand awareness. Branding your business takes time, but through consistent publicity where you're getting your name into the media, there's more of a chance for viewers, readers and consumers to recognize your brand, and then choose you over your competitors.*

In addition to raising brand awareness, publicity will also help you to increase your visibility and credibility as it allows you to spread your message to a large audience. When an individual receives publicity – whether through TV, radio, print or web – they are given an opportunity to connect with hundreds of viewers, readers and listeners, as well as potential customers." Pace Public Relations

The topics covered in this chapter are:

- ☐ Blog tours
  - ◦ Guest post ideas
  - ◦ Interview ideas
- ☐ Promotions
- ☐ Media
- ☐ Press releases

Blog Tours

Blog tours are an optional marketing task. They can be commissioned after the book launch, but the ideal time to run a blog tour is to have it straddle the launch date. That is , have some blog stops prior to the launch and some after the launch. This requires a degree of advanced planning. Whether you use a blog tour or not depends on your marketing budget. If you can afford it, a blog tour is a good way to get many people (i.e. potential buyers) to learn about your book.

Here is an explanation of a blog tour from the Penguin Random House web site: *A blog tour is a set amount of time, usually a week or two, in which your book will be promoted across various websites and blogs. The dates are set in advance; each blog knows what material it will be posting, and the content should be unique to each blog.*

Blog tours are not the same as writing blog posts for your own blog. In a blog tour, you are a guest on other peoples 'blogs. Blog tours are usually set up by a company who specializes in these tours and who have many blogger contacts. You can set one up yourself if you know a lot of bloggers, but it will require much effort and time to contact the bloggers and schedule the acceptances.

If you sign up for a blog tour, expect to pay a chunk of money for it. Refer to the budgeting information in Chapter 1. You will also have to invest a substantial block of time working on it. For instance, if the tour encompasses ten stops (i.e. blog sites), you will have to prepare ten separate blog posts, and these blog sites expect original material, not cut and paste exercises.

Some of the bloggers 'requests may include:

- ☐ An author interview. The blogger will generally provide a list of questions to answer.
- ☐ A scene or two from the book.
- ☐ Answers to a list of questions.
- ☐ A post on why you wrote the book and any problems you ran into.

The most important use for a blog tour is to get book reviews. Some blog tour operators specialize in them. For this activity, you will have to furnish the operator with a copies of your book. The operator will need one copy for each format: pdf, mobi and epub. The operator will then will furnish the book to the reviewer. Some bloggers won't review an ebook, only a print book although these types of request are getting rarer. To get timely reviews around the launch date, the blog tour will have to be commissioned a few moths before launch.

You can find blog tour operators by searching on the web. You can also ask other writers about their experiences with various operators. Use your LinkedIn groups for this research. Typically, once you sign up and pay, you'll be assigned a tour guide who will answer your questions, find the appropriate bloggers and establish dates for the tour.

Here is one caveat about blog tours. It won't do much good if the blog stops aren't appropriate for the book you wrote. If you wrote an adventure story, don't get involved with blog tour operators who specialize in romance blog tours, even if the price is reasonable. In this case, you'll have wasted your money because the visitors to your blog stops will have no interest in your book.

You should be aware that some clever blog tour operators run scams. These tour operators don't send out requests to bloggers: they simply use their own blog sites. For instance, if the tour operator offers a ten-stop tour, they'll create ten new blog sites and use them for the tours.

Technically, you are getting the ten stops you signed up for, except no one will visit the sites. This is because these ten blogs don't get any traffic. The only people who ever visit them are the authors who think they are on a grand promotional tour.

Guest Post Ideas

Many bloggers love having guests on their site. Guest posts are a great way to for others to learn about you and your book.

So the question you may have is this: What do I write about?

This is an open-ended question that really has no answer because you can write about virtually everything and anything. Almost! Fiction books and non-fiction books have much different kinds of acceptable blog posts. Non-fiction is easier to come with post ideas. You can blog about:

- ☐ The reason for writing the book.
- ☐ How you came to have the knowledge you put into the book.
- ☐ About material that didn't make it into the book.
- ☐ Expand on a topic in the book.

Novels on the other hand require much more creativity.

- ☐ Interview your characters, one at a time or a few at a time.
- ☐ Why is the theme of the book? Why?
- ☐ Is the main character based on someone you know?
- ☐ Is this the first book in a series?
- ☐ What's your next novel about?

I'm sure you get the idea by now. This is good time to begin writing some of these blog posts while you search for appropriate sites to query.

Interview Ideas

Some bloggers like to post interviews with authors. This is another good opportunity to expand your name recognition and social media reach. These bloggers may or may not have a list of interview questions they will expect you to answer. In many cases the list may have a large number of questions and you'll be required to select ten or twelve to answer. This, of course, keeps the interviews that show up on the blog from using the same questions every time and adds variety to the posts.

However, other bloggers will expect you to come up with your own interview questions. In this case, it is wise to create a list of questions and answers in a readily accessible file. The list should be long enough so that you can put together a number of different interviews for the bloggers.

Here are some questions and issues you can consider:

- ☐ Tell us about yourself.
- ☐ Why did you write this book?
- ☐ What do you want the reader to get from your book?
- ☐ What's different about your book?
- ☐ Where did the idea for the book come from?
- ☐ What's your next writing project?

You get the idea. Expand the list of questions and write the answers.

Promotions

If you budgeted for book promotions, it is best to start promoting the book before the launch date. But first you have to make a decision: how much are you willing to spend on a promotion? This is somewhat of a loaded question because promotions come in a number of flavors: inexpensive, moderately expensive and very expensive.

This task will require research on your part. I can provide some explanations and leads, but you will have to dig into the guts of other websites to find out all you can before committing money.

Some promotional sites are easy to understand and easy to use. Some, like Google Ads, are filled with techno-babble and are difficult to follow.

Generally, the more you spend, the bigger your reach (i.e the more potential readers you'll reach), but this isn't a hard and fast rule.

Promotional websites pop up continuously, and a web search will give you a list of sites to check on. Here is a link to a webpage that lists a hundred or more book promotion sites: https://www.readersintheknow.com/list-of-book-promotion-sites. The list contains a few sites that no longer exist, and I'm not recommending any sites in the list. Perform your due diligence in going through the list. Some of the sites will only promote free books. As a former sales manager, I don't understand the logic behind spending money to give away books. Some of these sites will only promote books that are available on Kindle.

Then there are promotional sites which are nothing but scams. It is in your best interest to read all the fine print before you commit money to a promotional site that looks suspicious. What does suspicious mean? For starters, if a site guarantees a certain number of book sales, it most certainly is suspicious. This is because, given the total flakiness of readers, no one can guarantee a level of sales. Before you commit money to any promotional site that hasn't been recommended to you, ask about it on your LinkedIn and Goodreads groups.

Costs

There are several different types of promotions. In one, you pay a flat fee to promote your book. With these, you fill in a data sheet with the title, author, description, price, buy links and the cover. The site sends out the information in an email or newsletter and (hopefully) people buy a copy of the book.

Most types of promotions are more complicated. First, you have to construct the ad. This usually consists of the book cover or the title and a very short sentence followed by a call-to-action (i.e. Buy Now!) and a link to a site selling your book.

The cost of the ad is a variable. In one version, you pay per thousand impressions. An impression is your ad showing up on some website. You hope the ad will result in viewers clicking on it. When they do, they are taken to a page selling your book. Typical prices are a dollar or two per thousand impressions and are usually fixed by the promotional site.

In a second version, you pay a fee every time someone clicks on your ad, but you aren't charged by the number of impressions. In these ads, the cost may be ten, twenty-five or fifty cents per click. The fee can also be higher or lower. In most case, you set the price you want to pay.

With either version, you construct the ad using a set of options. You can set a start and end date, a daily budget and a total budget. Depending on the length of the ad and the daily budget, these promotions can become expensive, so you have to monitor your spending closely. Google Ads (formerly Adwords) is typical of this type of promotional site. The success of these ad campaigns hinges on the keywords you select for the ad. Google has tools to help you select the correct ones.

The third — very expensive — kind of promotion involves hiring a promotion company to promote your book. These promotions will require you to sign a contract and pay up front. In return, the company will do an enormous amount of work promoting your book. Since there are large amounts of money involved here, make sure you do a lot of research before signing up with such a company. LinkedIn may be a good place to start your research.

Promo Sites

I've run a lot of book ads and here are some of the sites I've used or looked into.

When it comes to promotional companies, they are the very expensive ones mentioned earlier. I'm familiar with two of them: Smith Publicity and Author Marketing Expert

Smith Publicity https://www.smithpublicity.com is an international publicity company.

Author Marketing Expert https://www.amarketingexpert.com is run by Penny Sansevieri, who is considered a social media marketing guru.

In conclusion

Book promotions can be used to spread the word about your book and even sell copies. The promotions can also drain your wallet. Don't sign up with a promotional site without researching it. Once the promotion is running, monitor the results and especially your spending.

If you plan to use a promotion company contact them long before the launch date. It takes time for the company to complete the promotional work and you want the promotions to start prior to the launch of the book.

Contact the Media

This is another iffy thing you can do. When you send out a press release announcing the availability of your book, send a copy to the local paper. A word of caution, copy and paste the release into the body of the email, don't make it an attachment. An attachment won't be opened and your email will be deleted unread. You can usually find an email address on the paper's website. Be prepared to be ignored.

Having a book published these days isn't a big news event. It happens all the time now, so your book won't make a big splash in the local paper world.

Don't be discouraged. Remember, when your first book is launched, you are an unknown and papers don't like to publish reports on unknowns (unless you have also pulled off a despicable crime). The approach to use is to keep writing press releases (for new reviews, etc.) and keep sending a copy to local papers. This has the result that reporters keep seeing your name pop up from time to time and someday (perhaps!) one of them will get in touch with you.

Since having a book published is no longer newsworthy, another tactic you can use is to combine a book event with a local interest angle. This is much more likely to get a reporter's interest.

Radio and TV are other media outlets to address. Many stations look for authors and writers to contact them to help fill up air time with interviews. Granted, getting interviewed when you have little or no name recognition is difficult, but you have to start sometime. Getting the first one is always the hardest. After that, your query letter can list the first one as proof that you are an interesting character who should be interviewed.

One place to start searching for media interviews is Blog Talk Radio https://www.blogtalkradio.com. It has many talk shows that are eager to interview authors and is perhaps the easiest way to get a media interview. All the shows are recorded and are available to be listened to or downloaded as podcasts long after the live event. You'll have to search through the site to find the appropriate show hosts and then send them a query email describe your book and yourself.

Press Release
There are a number of sites that will issue your press release. Do a web search to locate a few. Some of them are free. Some charge a modest fee and some are expensive. Generally, the more you pay, the bigger and more prestigious the media outlets contacted.

The purpose of the press release is to tell media sites about the availability of your book. The press release service will distribute the announcement to a large number of media companies.

The press releases sites will have a template or instructions you can use to compose the release.

Press releases start with a short, attention-grabbing headline followed by a longer, but still short, blurb. After that comes the main text area where you can describe your book in depth. This is another place where the short synopsis is useful. Your book cover image also goes into the release as does your short bio and buy links. If you have a trailer, include the link to it.

Once the release has gone out, get a copy and send it to your local media outlets. You may get a write-up, and that will help your marketing efforts.

Here are links to a few press release sites:

PRLog: https://www.prlog.org

PRweb: https://app.prweb.com

Chapter 8: Advertising

Introduction

The goal of advertising is to get more people to know about your book and, hopefully, to buy a copy of it.

This chapter will cover the following topics:

- ☐ Books Go Social
- ☐ Bookgorilla
- ☐ Fussy Librarian
- ☐ Bookbub
- ☐ Facebook ads boost
- ☐ Amazon Marketing Services
- ☐ Google ads
- ☐ Readers in the Know
- ☐ Independent Author Network
- ☐ Bookbuzzr

Ads are hard to get a handle on. Do they sell books? That is a difficult or even impossible question to answer, but the answer could be a negative. Are they worth the effort and the cost? Yet another question that can't be answered. Will they sell enough books to recover the ad cost? Rarely, but it is possible. The only clear thing about ads is that they can cost a bucket of money.

There are many different type of ads. I'm sure you're familiar with the print ads in newspapers and magazines, not to mention the ads on the Internet. It's difficult to find a web page that doesn't have an ad buried on it someplace or has an ad that tries to distract you from reading whatever your went to the web page to see. Perhaps the only website that is ad-free is my website. I refuse to allow ads on it.

Webpage ads are sold by size and shape. They come in banner shapes and tower shapes and they come in various size text boxes. No matter the shape, their common measurement is pixels. A pixel is a pretty small unit of measurement and there are 75 to an inch. Besides text and possibly a small graphic, these ads have an embedded target link. The price of these ads is based on the size and the page placement because some webpage real estate is more valuable than other places on the page. Many of these ads will cost a flat rate, usually per week or per month while others are priced on the clicks .

If you intend to use ads, don't waste your money by buying space on an inappropriate webpage. A website selling guns and sporting gear is no place for an ad about a romance novel.

Print ads such as newspaper and magazine ads are expensive. How expensive are they? An eighth of a page ad in the Book Section of the New York Times costs $2500. That's for an ad that runs once. Generally, the bigger and more prestigious the newspaper or magazine, the more the ad will cost. The ad's cost is also proportional to the paper or magazine's circulation and the size of the ad.

So let's talk about some sites that I'm familiar with. There are many, many more than my list, but my remarks will be limited to this few. They are typical of what you'll find on the web.

Books Go Social

https://booksgosocial.com is a site that will promote your books using a variety of web tools depending on the level of service you order. It also offers publishing services and training courses.

Bookgorilla

Bookgorilla uses a daily email sent to a large list of subscribers to tell them about discounted or free ebooks available on Kindle. You can find it here: https://www.bookgorilla.com

The Fussy Librarian

The Fussy Librarian is another site that will advertise your ebook. You can find it here: https://www.thefussylibrarian.com

It works the same way most of these sites work: you commission the ad for your book, pay the fee and then the site sends out the information in an email blast. Some sites send the email out daily and others send it weekly. This site sends it daily for reduced price books and on days you pick for free ebooks.

I can never understand the need to pay for an ad for a free ebook.

Bookbub

https://www.bookbub.com/launch is a big site that has two types of promotions: very expensive email lists and pay per click. Their email lists are extensive and Bookbub is very selective about whom they allow to advertise, even if you're willing to pay the fee. You can submit your book free of charge and you'll be informed if it's selected or not. If your book is selected, you pay the fee (think a minimum of $800 or $900 dollars: it keeps going up!) The higher the price of your book during the promotion, the greater the fee. If selected, you will sell a lot of books. Will it cover the cost of the campaign? I don't know. I've used Bookbub several times in the past, but that was when it first started out and the fee was a hundred bucks or so. The site became wildly successful, and the prices shot through the roof and it became very tough to get selected.

Bookbub also has pay per click campaigns you can use. They work similar to Google Ads.

Facebook Boost and Ads

Once you start a Facebook Page for your book, you can add posts to the page to keep followers up to date on your activities or on book sales. If you have a number of people following the page, say 250, it's logical to expect your post to be seen by all 250 followers but you're wrong. Facebook will show it to only a handful of followers and give you the option of *boosting* the post by paying Facebook for this service. There are a number of options as to the length of the boost, the overall budget and how much your willing to pay each day.

Facebook also has ads that can be used to promote a product such as your book.

Amazon Marketing Services

If your book is on Amazon, you can use its Amazon Marketing Services: https://advertising.amazon.com. Amazon has several options available including pay per click and other types of ad campaigns.

A confusing point about the campaign reports is they show the revenue Amazon takes in from the campaign, not your royalties. So at first blush, it will look like your campaign is much more successful than it really is.

The key to success with Amazon Marketing services is to launch many ads at the same time, all using a different keyword. This can become a tedious and time-consuming chore. To learn more about running AMS ads on your own, you can take this free course: https://kindlepreneur.com/ams-book-advertising-course/

Author Mark Cain says this about Amazon Marketing Services: *I'm an Amazon exclusive writer, and I like AMS because it's point-of-sale marketing. People who click on Amazon ads are looking for a book to buy. For AMS I hire out developing and managing my Amazon ads to a person who understands the Amazon system much better than I do.*

If you decide to use AMS, it may be wise to do what Mark does: find someone to run the ads for you.

One such company is Resurrecting Books: https://www.resurrectingbooks.com. It's run by Michal Stawicki and both Mark Cain and I have used Michal's company with good results.

Google Ads

Google ads are similar to Amazon Marketing Services in that they use keyword driven ads trying to get people to click on the embedded link. Like Amazon Marketing Services, success depends upon the relevance of the keywords and the number of keywords used.

Readers in the Know

Readers in the Know is site that is substantially different from the others. It's a website where you can upload your book cover and blurb. This requires starting an account and a fee. You can use the site to advertise your book promotions on other websites.

It also maintain a list of promotional sites with links. Here is a link to the webpage: https://www.readersintheknow.com/list-of-book-promotion-sites

The last time I looked, a few sites were defunct.

The Independent Author Network

This is a large site consisting of many self-published authors. You can find the site here: https://www.independentauthornetwork.com

You can add your books to the site after you set up an author page. It'll promote your book for a fee.

Bookbuzzr

Bookbuzzr is a book marketing site. The site can be found here: http://www.bookbuzzr.com. The site offers to promote your book or books for a monthly fee. It also has a suite of services it offers to authors.

Chapter 9: What Other Authors Say

Introduction

While writing an early draft of this book, I contacted a dozen other authors I know and asked them if they would answer a few questions about how they market their books. Most of them agreed and replied to my questions. (I answered the questions also). Their answers are amazing in their diversity. No two of the replies were close to being similar.

Here are the questions:

1: What is your favorite or most successful marketing tactic?

2: How do you use it?

3: Would you recommend it for newbies?

4: What is your least favorite or least successful marketing tactic?

5: If you could recommend one marketing tactic for newbie book marketers, what would it be?

The authors who responded are (along with a link to their Amazon page):

Mark Cain: https://www.amazon.com/Mark-Cain/e/B00EBB8PG0%3Fref=dbs_a_mng_rwt_scns_share

Elizabeth Craig: https://www.amazon.com/Elizabeth-Spann-

Craig/e/B0024J8X04

Karen Cavalli: https://www.amazon.com/Karen-Cavalli/e/B014PLY3FC/ref=dp_byline_cont_pop_ebooks_1

Stuart Aken: https://www.amazon.co.uk/Stuart-Aken/e/B002WTJ3VE?ref=sr_ntt_srch_lnk_1&qid=1590068527&sr=8-1

Lorraine Ash: https://www.amazon.com/Lorraine-Ash/e/B001KCH4R4%3Fref=dbs_a_mng_rwt_scns_share

Peadar O'Guilin:
https://www.amazon.co.uk/s?k=peadar+o+guilin&i=digital-text&crid=29BCZBSA6FONR&sprefix=Peadar+%2Cdigital-text%2C214&ref=nb_sb_ss_ts-a-p_1_7

Nicolette Pierce: https://www.amazon.com/Nicolette-Pierce/e/B008LBR0JO%3Fref=dbs_a_mng_rwt_scns_share

L. Diane Wolfe: https://www.amazon.com/L-Diane-Wolfe/e/B002C1X7XC?ref=sr_ntt_srch_lnk_3&qid=1590068933&sr=1-3

Stephenie Auteri: https://www.amazon.com/Steph-Auteri/e/B076CTSKV4/ref=dp_byline_cont_ebooks_1

Hank Quense: https://www.amazon.com/-/e/B002BM76IE

Nanci Arvizu: www.nanciwrites.com

Questions 1 to 3
in this section, I combined the answers to the first three questions.

The questions are:

- ☐ What is your favorite or most successful marketing tactic?
- ☐ How do you use it?
- ☐ Would you recommend it for newbies?

Mark Cain:

What is your favorite or most successful marketing tactic?

I can't reduce it to one. I have three or four.

A. Developing an eye-catching cover.

B. Writing a good book description.

C. Using Amazon Marketing Services. I'm an Amazon exclusive writer, and I like AMS because it's point-of-sale marketing. People who click on Amazon ads are looking for a book to buy.

Conceptually, I also like search engine optimization (SEO), where you use the right combination of words in your book description, title, keywords and categories to rank high in an Amazon search. It's hard to do, and doesn't always work, but discoverability on Amazon is key to selling.

How do you use it?

I hire out developing and managing my Amazon ads to a person who understands the amazon system much better than I do. He develops hundreds of ads per book, and he develops ads for three different marketplaces, amazon.com, amazon.co.uk and amazon.ca.

Would you recommend it for newbies?

Yes, I'd recommend the service for newbies. There is a challenge, though, in knowing enough to develop successful ads. I used to do my own, but I was an amateur at it. Outsourcing this function has worked better for me, and allowed me to focus on other aspects of writing and publishing.

Elizabeth Craig:

What is your favorite or most successful marketing tactic?

My favorite and I feel most-successful marketing tactic is the Goodreads Giveaway. I do the $119 one.

How do you use it?

I use the giveaway to add awareness of and visibility for my series. If I have a new release coming up, I'll run a giveaway for the first book of the series. The giveaway is for as many as 100 ebooks, although you can give away as few as 10. Goodreads handles everything: they notify the winners and distribute the ebooks. I pay for the giveaway through my Amazon account. The coolest thing is that everyone who enters the giveaway has my book added to their "want to read" list, which also shows up in their friends' feeds on the site. You may end up netting more reviews, as well, since Goodreads sends a reminder to the winners after 8 weeks to rate and review the title. Reviews, of course, also help with visibility.

Instead of the Goodreads' recommended 1-month listing, you'll be in Goodreads' "recently listed" and "ending soon" alerts if you keep the giveaway length fairly short.

Would you recommend it for newbies?

I do recommend the giveaway for newbies as it's fairly easy to figure out. You start out here: https://www.goodreads.com/giveaway/show_create_options. On the other hand, it's not the cheapest investment in the world. If your books aren't known yet, you may want to make sure you either promote the giveaway on your social media outlets or consider a less-expensive option.

Karen Cavalli:

What is your favorite or most successful marketing tactic?

Connecting personally with readers and potential readers (my favorite and most successful).

How do you use it?

Pre-COVID-19 I connected in-person with readers and potential readers by holding public talks, being interviewed for talk radio, offering classes, and, when I could, attending conferences and renting a vendor table. Now I connect digitally — I still do the interviews for talk radio and podcasts since they were and are often done virtually; videos, social media posts and blog tours (June 7 starts a blog tour for my next book, a paranormal romance). I'm offering two writer workshops virtually in July and August of this year, and I'm trying to figure out how I can offer signed copies of my work during the live session. People like the signed copies!

Would you recommend it for newbies?

Definitely!

Stuart Aken:

What is your favorite or most successful marketing tactic?

Difficult. I spent a year as a sales rep, many years ago, and the experience left me with a deep distrust of all sales talk and techniques. I learned how much cheating, lying and exaggeration goes on in the field. As someone who's always loved honesty and truth, I now find it hard to associate myself with marketing and promotion. However, I want people to read my work, so I take the route of least activity: I list my work on my website, do very occasional tweets and Facebook posts relating quotes from reviews of my books, and have attended the launches of my books, which have usually been at an annual convention run by my publisher. Whilst there, I also work on the book stall to sell other books published by my publisher.

How do you use it?

I think that's answered above.

Would you recommend it for newbies?

I'd recommend setting up a website, and an author page on Goodreads and Amazon, as soon as possible, simply to let potential readers know you exist.

Lorraine Ash:

What is your favorite or most successful marketing tactic?

A mix of tactics is crucial — personal appearances, a home state media tour, and online outreach. I n all cases the goal is to get people talking about your book. Word-of-mouth recommendations are the only thing that sells books.

How do you use it?

- Posting quality content about the book's story and insights in specialized social media groups and engaging in the discussions the posts generate;
- Sitting for interviews with quality podcasters who explore the same themes and issues: their present audiences and your potential readership probably overlap;
- Creating a newsy, friendly, accessible author website designed to invite conversation and capture addresses for an email list;
- Presenting book readings and Q-and-A sessions via Zoom through such groups as the Quarantine Book Club.

Would you recommend it for newbies?

Yes, because these methods are both efficacious and low cost. They do not depend on celebrity and they help create and grow readership.

Peadar O'Guilin:

What is your favorite or most successful marketing tactic?

I am genuinely very poor at marketing. However, a few things do work for me in a small way. Every person we meet for the first time, is part of at least one large network of people that does not include us. Sometimes, it can pay to give away a book for free in these circumstances. For example, when my publisher sent me a dozen copies of the Polish translation of one of my books, I made a point of sending one to a colleague in an office in Poland. He may never have read it himself, but soon everybody in that building knew I was a writer with books available in their language.

Similarly, my email signature always contains a reference to my books, so that even a note sent to my bank will work for me as a form of advertising

How do you use it?

See above.

Would you recommend it for newbies?

Absolutely! The hard sell will always put people off, but letting the world know your book exists is vital.

Nicolette Pierce:

What is your favorite or most successful marketing tactic?

I've found third party newsletters to be useful, relatively inexpensive, and effective.

How do you use it?

There are many newsletters to choose from. Start by researching them as a reader and find the ones that would best suit your book. This tactic generally works best when you have a first in series book marked as free. But many authors have been successful using other pricing strategies with it.

Would you recommend it for newbies?

Yes, but as with all marketing, just be mindful of how you spend your money. Talk to fellow authors about which newsletters worked best for them. Great places to find this information is in author groups on Facebook . Some newsletters that work great today might not be great tomorrow. And what works for one author might not work for you.

L. Diane Wolfe:

What is your favorite or most successful marketing tactic?

One of our favorites is marketing to libraries. They have several distinct advantages – libraries don't return books, they have to replace books as they are worn out which leads to more sales, they introduce readers to new authors, and they are great places for authors to hold events or make appearances.

How do you use it?

We have a large database of libraries, both in the USA and around the world. With each of our authors, we compose an author sheet that highlights the following: their professional qualities, organizations, awards, and areas of expertise; their speaking topics; select videos and podcasts; other publications; and their new book and reviews. We also compose a book sell sheet that lists all of the book's information, including how to order. Starting 1-4 weeks before its release, we email the two items to libraries. This results in libraries both stocking the book and inviting the author in for an appearance if local.

Would you recommend it for newbies?

If they are comfortable with appearances, it's the perfect way to get in front of potential readers and generate book sale

Stephanie Auteri:

What is your favorite or most successful marketing tactic?

I don't know that I can qualify this as my favorite, as it's also the one that terrifies me the most, but in-person events can be incredibly useful in moving books, especially when you don't have the type of high-profile book that's landing on best-of lists or getting reviewed in the biggest publications.

And I don't mean straight single-author readings. First-time, low-profile authors are going to have a tough time getting people to show up for an event like this if people don't already know you and/or your work. Think about how you can provide added value to attendees. Show up in conversation with another, higher-profile author or industry professional. Teach a workshop at a literary festival. Give a session at a conference. End up as the main speaker at an event that is somehow connected to the topic of your book. Or maybe even participate in an already-established reading series, where multiple authors are reading. Things like these have built-in audiences.

Much to my surprise, I've found that if I can get myself in front of a group of people, I can then win them over with my writing or with my knowledge base or with my boundless charm and then they end up clamoring to buy my book.

How do you use it?

Oh crap, I think I already answered this above.

Would you recommend it for newbies?

I'd absolutely recommend it for newbies. Especially for newbies.

Particularly since newbies might not be given the same marketing and promotional opportunities as higher-profile authors.

Hank Quense:

What is your favorite or most successful marketing tactic?

My favorite tactic is getting reviews. Another favorite is to sell books at events such as library lectures. The lecture topic may be non-fiction but folks tend to buy the fiction books along with the non-fiction books

How do you use it?

Granted, reviews are not easy to get, but once I do get a 4 or 5 star review, I spread the word about the review using social media. For lectures, I contact libraries, introduce myself and ask if I can hold a lecture there. Even if the library doesn't pay me a speaking fee, I have the opportunity to sell copies of my print books

Would you recommend it for newbies?

Definitely. There are many useful sites that will help an author get reviews. For a fee. Lectures, however, require the author to stand in front of strangers and talk. Many people are terrified of doing that so this one many not be for everyone

Nanci Arvizu:

What is your favorite or most successful marketing tactic?

For my budget and time, podcast interviews. Being a guest can be free if you trade your time for finding shows. Or pay someone else/find a service that connects hosts, shows and guests.

It's as easy as having a conversation with someone who is asking questions about something you already know you, your story and your book. there's not a lot of prep work involved. Make sure you have the right soft-ware, quiet space to record, your time zones right and you know how to log in to the show. There's nothing more nerve racking, for you and the host, than to be late.

How do you use it?

I have my own podcast and reach out to be a guest on other shows. Then I write about the experience, what I learned and maybe something that happened behind the scenes, because that happens a lot.

Doing too many shows, my own or others, can be a time vampire. It takes away from the time I could/should be writing. So now I limit both. When I was hosting Page Readers I wasn't focused on my own writing and I over loaded myself with guests, shows and all the prep-work. Burnout was inevitable and I learned a lesson: I don't want to be be tied to a microphone.

Balance between all three is required for me to feel like I'm making progress with the big picture of writing, podcasting, and playing golf (aka, having a life).

Would you recommend it for newbies?

Absolutely. It's as easy as having a conversation! Get your info together and be comfortable telling your story. Be sure your voice is good too! No one wants to listen to someone cough or constantly clearing their throat through an interview. It's really hard on the interviewer too.

Then be prepared to share it! This is no different that having a book published by the big guys. They're not in charge of publicity unless you're already a superstar. So the social media, media, public relations, sending flyers to your moms quilting club, is all up to you.

So don't screw it up! Everyone you know will be listening!

No pressure.

Question 4

What is your least favorite or least successful marketing tactic?

Mark Cain:

The use of social media. I feel particularly strongly about Facebook, in which I've invested way too much time over the years for too little payback. I have yet to do facebook ads, though. Their cost is high, and I have yet to be convinced of their efficacy.

Elizabeth Craig:

I feel ads are the most time-consuming and highest learning-curve option for promo. Each ad opportunity (whether BookBub, Facebook, or Amazon) operates slightly differently. To make sure you don't lose money, I'd highly recommend taking either a paid or a free course (Reedsy offers some: https://blog.reedsy.com/learning/courses/). And to really do it right, you should compare different versions of an ad and different audiences. As an English major, I've found it very tough-going.

Stuart Aken:

I've never measured activity, so I can't answer this in terms of success. But my least favourite activity is the whole spectrum of sales. I long for the days when publishers did all the marketing and promotional work, and left authors free to create the work. It's the creation that matters to me.

Lorraine Ash:

Following the online theme, any endeavor that is taken over by a computer algorithm or function instead of a human. I've been involved in many expert online ad campaigns, some of them quite expensive. Results have always looked great in terms of numbers of impressions and clicks, but not in books sold. They don't necessarily convert to sales. People engage people. Machines do not.

Peadar O'Guilin:

Constant bombardment. Begging. As a regular book purchaser, I need to feel that when I buy a book it's because it was my own choice.

Nicolette Pierce:

Direct sales or direct promotion to my fans. I'm not very good at promoting my own work without an ad platform. I know this about myself, so I rely heavily on other tactics such as newsletters, AMS ads, Facebook ads, etc.

L. Diane Wolfe:

Bookstore appearances used to be all the rage and they can be a lot of fun, but there is the downside of book returns. We do send the same author and book sheets to book stores, but we caution our authors that if they do a book signing or event, make sure the stores don't order too many books and sign any that remain after the event.

(Because those can't be returned.) Plus, so many stores just don't host events anymore.

Stephanie Auteri:

I set up a Facebook author page because my publisher asked me to. But I felt so lackluster about it — partially because it felt forced, partially because I was already so engaged on other platforms — that it remained mostly stagnant. To be clear, I'm not saying that you shouldn't create a Facebook author page. What I am saying is that you don't need to be on every single social media platform out there. Consider where your target audience is hanging out. Consider which platforms you're most active on and comfortable with. The goal is engagement and if you're not naturally engaged and engaging on a platform, it's going to be a dud for you.

Hank Quense:

Anything on Facebook. Boosting posts or buying ads on Facebook are complicated and don't produce anything useful. The reports aren't user-friendly either and difficult to interpret.

Nanci Arvizu:

Facebook. I've seen authors run successful campaigns, but they've usually got a wizard behind the curtain running those ads, requiring a budget, like, real money, and a lot of authors aren't in the position to take the financial plunge this could become if they don't set it up right.

Question 5

If you could recommend one marketing tactic for newbie book marketers, what would it be?

Mark Cain:

Make your covers and book descriptions eye catching.

Elizabeth Craig:

My top marketing tip is for writers to have an online "home": a website. Industry expert Jane Friedman has solid tips for a first site: https://www.janefriedman.com/author-websites/

Karen Cavalli:

Keep top of mind to connect with those are likely to be drawn in by your work. This sounds so basic, but I find it takes work figuring out where potential readers are going to hang out, whether through digital or analog means. And then figure out how best to reach them.

Stuart Aken:

I think every author needs to have at least a presence online. Whether that's a website, an author page, or a social media presence is up to the individual. But I'd give a warning regarding social media: writers, as a group, are generally interested in a multitude of things. It is too easy to become embroiled in online discussions about social/political issues that matter to you. Beware: such activity can devour much of the time you should be using to write!

Lorraine Ash:

Put up a killer website. Don't rely on a Facebook page. The first thing people do when they hear about your book — or you — is go to your website. If you don't have one, they figure you're somehow not legit. If you do have one, you give yourself multiple opportunities to engage with them, page after page.

Peadar O'Guilin:

Read and review lots of other people's books. Don't push your own work when you do, but have a link there for the curious.

Nicolette Pierce:

Probably the third party newsletter because it is the easiest. But with everything, it comes with trial and error. Keep good notes and watch your sales reports. It will help indicate if your strategy is working or not.

L. Diane Wolfe:

We recommend the library market for any author who is not afraid of speaking in public or who wants sales without returns. Even if the library just stocks the eBook, that's still sales.

Stephanie Auteri:

Build your platform before you land your book deal, and immediately build a mailing list that's connected with it. If you wait until your book's done, it's too late. Building a community of people who give a crap about you and what you have to say takes time. Building that brand loyalty takes time. You want people to be excited about your book before it comes out. Then, you can use that platform and that mailing list to keep people updated on what's coming down the pike and, if they're a loyal and enthusiastic and engaged community of fans, not only will they buy your book, but they'll also recommend it to their friends and followers.

Hank Quense:

I would recommend spending time on getting reviews.. Give ebooks away to friends and family. Give them away to anyone who agrees to write a review. Keep in mind thought less than half of the strangers who get a free copy will actually write a review..

Nanci Arvizu:

Build your own author website NOW. If you haven't already, do it now. Set up a blog and post to it. The ebbs and flows of it over time won't matter, you'll always have it to show growth, keep track of projects, links to other sites, awards, news articles about your work. You might even post a blog entry now and then. Keep it no matter what, even when you think you don't want it anymore. Sites like Contently and Medium are great, but they're not yours.

Chapter 10: More stuff

Websites
Penny Sansevieri: Author Marketing Experts:
https://www.amarketingexpert.com
Rachael Thompson: https://rachelintheoc.com
Sandra Beckwith: https://buildbookbuzz.com
Joanna Penn: https://www.thecreativepenn.com

Books
The Secrets to Ebook Publishing Success by Mark Coker
Smashwords Book Marketing Guide by Mark Coker
Red Hot Internet Publicity by Penny Sansevieri
30-Day Marketing Challenge by Rachael Thompson
How to Self-publish and Market a Book by Hank Quense

SWOT Analysis
SWOT stands for Strengths, Weaknesses, Opportunities and Threats. The SWOT analysis is a standard way to identify the problems in a set of circumstances.

Here is the Wikipedia definition: *SWOT analysis is a strategic planning technique used to help a person or organization identify strengths, weaknesses, opportunities, and threats related to business competition or project planning.*

In the situation addressed by this book, SWOT means the state of affairs facing an author who wishes to market a book for the first time.

I've created a SWOT chart for newbie book marketeers. It may be helpful to review the situation you face. The SWOT analysis isn't meant to discourage you. It depicts the facts and offers suggestions on how to face up to this real world situation. You can view the SWOT chart (as well as other interesting material) using this link:

http://hankquense.org/wp/writers-and-authors-resource-center/

Scams

As an author, especially a newly self-published one, you will be subjected to a barrage of "helpful" offers. Some of the offers will be legitimate and some will be from scam artists. How did all these people find you? Your book is on the internet and so is your name as the book's author. It doesn't take much research for others to find out you're self-published and that this is your first book. Consider this as your initial taste of fame. Once the parties have identified you as a first-time self-publisher, they'll start targeting you with offers to help. Some of them will come by email, others will come via direct messages on social media sites.

Below, I'll discuss a few scams I've come across. These are illustrative examples. There are many more, and new ones pop up all the time because the scammers are very creative.

Be warned. The marketing swamp can be hazardous to your financial health.

Marketing help

One of the most prevalent scams is an email with a link to an impressive-looking website that describes an incredible way to get your book in front of vast hordes of readers who have been waiting for a book like yours. And they will be willing to help you market your book for only a 'small 'consideration.

Be careful when investigating a book marketing service that places ads on other website or sends out emails. Many of these come from scammers who will 'offer 'a package of services that will cost an arm and a leg. Check out the service on your LinkedIn and Goodreads groups.

Your account is locked

This is a tacky one. You'll get an email claiming an account you have (like PayPal) has been locked and you need to send your personal information to get it unlocked. One way to uncover this type of scam is to right click or hover the mouse arrow on the email address. If it looks nothing like the site it claims to be from, it's a genuine scam. Delete it and don't click on any links in the body of the email.

Your domain name will expire shortly

Your domain name must be renewed annually, which gives rise to this scam operation. This is typically done with snail mail (you have to give your home address when you register a domain name, and domain name registration information is public information). The letter will tell you that your domain name is in danger of being lost if it isn't renewed before it expires.

As a courtesy, the operator will renew it for you for a small charge of perhaps $50 or $100 per domain name. They'll even offer a reduced price to extend the domain name for several years, payable in advance.

Whatever server you use will tell you when the domain name has to be renewed. My domain names are registered through my server, *A Small Orange* and they advise me in advance when the domain name will expire. Mine are automatically renewed as part of the service provided by ASO and it costs $15 per year per domain name.

Throw these offers in the recycling.

Contests

It's imperative that you read the fine print and the FAQs on each contest website. One time I received an email about a contest I hadn't heard about. In reading the FAQs, I came across a statement that said the judges do not read all entries. They pick and choose which ones to read. Say what? Why would an author enter a contest and pay a fee of perhaps a $100 if there is a good chance the book wouldn't be read. In looking at the lists of winners from the previous contests, I was struck by the number of awards that went to books published by a vanity press house with a very unsavory reputation. To me, the winner's list screamed collusion. My advice is always read everything you can about the contests before committing money.

Email Blasts

This one will offer to tell tens of thousands of people about your book via an email announcement. And it only costs a few hundred dollars, which comes out to pennies per announcement. Such a deal! The thing is, ninety-nine point ninety-nine percent of the emails sent out will never be read by the recipients. Most will be ignored or rerouted to the junk mail folder.

A variation on this involves Twitter, Facebook and other websites. For a small fee, the sender will get you a thousand followers. Unfortunately, the followers will have no interest in you or your book.

Book Seller Websites

I found this site when a friend asked me if I used it to sell books. I don't remember the name of the site, but it probably has gone out of business by now. At the site, you could upload a pdf edition of your book and the cover along with the blurb and other information, and the site would produce a web page for the book and display it. It looked attractive, but keep in mind that sites like this will never be a primary sales channel like Kindle, Barnes & Noble, iStore and the others. This is a secondary channel that may sell a book or two occasionally. I checked the revenue distribution and saw that it was 70/30 like Smashwords and Kindle. So far, so good. I did some more checking and the situation went downhill. Fast. The site distributes your royalties to you only after it accumulates a hundred dollars. So, if your book sells for $2.99, your cut will be $2.09. To reach a hundred dollars in sales you'll have to sell forty-eight copies of the book. Through a secondary channel like this, it will take years to accumulate a hundred dollars. The site meanwhile keeps the sales revenue it has collected from your book. And then I read the clincher: to display a book on the site will cost you a hundred dollars per book per year! The amazing thing to me was the large number of books the site displayed. Apparently, those authors didn't understand simple arithmetic or never bothered to read the conditions posted on the site. Always read all the information posted on sites before you agree to use that site. The information isn't always easy to find. Search the FAQs pages and all the other pages on the site. You never know where an interesting tidbit may be buried deep in the hope readers will stop reading before reaching the information.

Blog Tour Operators

Some clever tour operators don't send out requests to bloggers: they simply use their own blog sites. For instance, if the tour operator offers a ten-stop tour, they'll create ten new blog sites and use them for the tours.

Technically, you are getting the ten stops you signed up for, except no one will visit the sites. This is because these ten blogs don't get any traffic. The only people who ever visit them are the authors who think they are on a grand promotional tour.

Vanity Presses

Vanity presses are out to grab as much of your money as they possibly can. They don't care about you or your book. But don't take my word for it. Here's a link to an informative article about vanity presses and other scams you may run into.
https://blog.reedsy.com/scams-and-publishing-companies-to-avoid/

Here's another exercise for you to do: run a web search using the term 'vanity press.' Make sure you read a few of the myriad of articles that show up in the search results.

Remember

Always be vigilant! It's your money at risk!

My Marketing Plan

I guess it's only fair that disclose how I plan to market this book. At the present time (3 moths before the launch date) I have a preliminary plan that will be expanded as the big date nears.

I tend to make plans using mind-maps. Below is a graphic depicting my current (preliminary) plan.

I expand them as ideas come to me and implement them over time. Currently, I have one article to be published on a popular blog site. It will be available the same week as the launch.

Podcasts I'm not sure about. I have never done one and I don't listen to them, but it's an area I intend to explore.

From the graphic, you can see much of my focus will be on articles and getting book reviews. I have a half-dozen ideas for unique articles and I'll start soliciting reviews as soon as the book gets a web

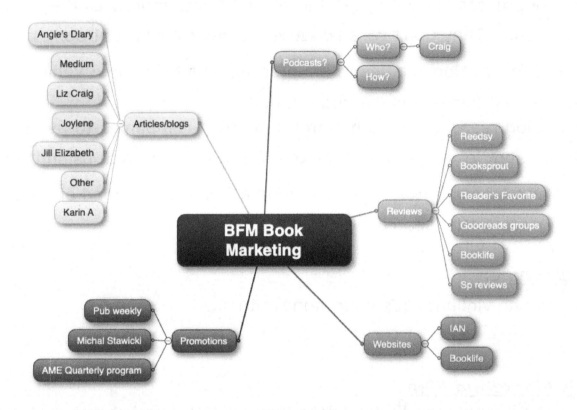

presence.

The names under articles are either article publishing sites or the names of bloggers I know. This listing will be expanded before long.

Chapter 11: About the author

Hank Quense writes humorous and satiric sci-fi and fantasy stories. He also writes and lectures about fiction writing and self-publishing. He has published 19 books and 50 short stories along with dozens of articles. He often lectures on fiction writing and publishing and has a series of guides covering the basics on each subject. He and his wife Pat usually vacation in another galaxy or parallel universe. They also time travel occasionally when Hank is searching for new story ideas.

Other books by Hank Quense

Fiction:
Gundarland Stories
Tales From Gundarland

Falstaff's Big Gamble

Wotan's Dilemma

The King Who Disappeared
Princess Moxie Series

Moxie's Problem

Moxie's Decision

Queen Moxie
Zaftan Troubles Series
Contact
Confusion
Combat

Convolution
Sam
Klatze
Gongeblazn

Non-fiction:
Fiction Writing Workshops for Kids
Business Basics for Authors
Creating Stories
Planning a Novel, Script or Memoir
How to Self-publish and Market a Book

You can buy any of these books on the websites of all major book sellers.

Links? You want links? Here you go:

Hank's website: http://hankquense.org/wp

Hank's Facebook fiction page:
https://www.facebook.com/StrangeWorldsOnline?ref=hl

Twitter: https://twitter.com/hanque99

LinkedIn: https://www.linkedin.com/in/hanque/

Instagram: https://www.instagram.com/hankquense/

Goodreads:
https://www.goodreads.com/author/show/3002079.Hank_Quense

Hank has been writing stories for over 20 years. He's been self-publishing for over ten. He also has been lecturing for more than ten years. Over time, he's created a wealth of material on these topics and has often considered collecting it all to build a library of sorts for writers and authors who were looking for advice.

He finally did it. He established a separate section on his website dedicated to all this material. Much of it has been previously published and some of it is new, created expressly for this new project.

You can find the main page for this collection here: http://hankquense.org/wp/writers-and-authors-resource-center/

Chapter 12: Index

Index of marketing tasks and information

Twitter chats
Video chats
Online launch party
Book giveaways
Physical book events

Chapter 7: Publicity: page 66

Blog tours
Guest post ideas
Interview ideas
Promotions
Contact the media
Press release

Chapter 8: Advertising: page 76

Books Go Social
Bookgorilla
Fussy Librarian
Bookbub
Facebook ads
Amazon Marketing Services
Google ads
Readers in the Know
Independent Author Network
Bookbuzzr

Chapter 9: What Other Authors Say: page 81

List of authors

Favorite Tactic
Least favorite
Recommended tactic

Chapter10: More Stuff: page 96

Additional resources
Scams
My marketing plan

Last Words of Advice:

Book marketing is hard. It requires a lot of time and money. nevertheless, it is an activity you must engage in if you wish to sell books. And why wouldn't you want to sell books?

So, suck it up and plunge in: market your book.

Don't be overwhelmed by the sheer number of tasks listed in this book. Remember, you don't have to start all of them at once.

YOU CAN DO THIS!

Made in United States
North Haven, CT
07 May 2022

18997800R00063